THE TERROR OF ETTINMARSH

By Che Webster

CLASSIC FANTASY © 2016 by The Design Mechanism
MYTHRAS is a Trademark of The Design Mechanism.

All rights reserved. This edition of The Terror of Ettinmarsh is copyright © 2017.
This book may not be reproduced in whole or in part by any means without permission from The Design Mechanism, except as quoted for purposes of illustration, discussion and game play. Reproduction of the material in this book for the purposes of personal or corporate profit, by photographic, electronic, or other methods of retrieval is strictly prohibited.

Published under license in the UK by Aeon Games Publishing
www.aeongamespublishing.co.uk

ISBN 978-1-91147-126-4

Printed in Great Britain

Contents

Credits

Written by Che Webster

Art by Jethro Lentle and Jeremy Hart

Cartography by Colin Driver and Ronan Salieri

Project Manager: Rodney Leary

Editor: Brian Pivik

Layout: Alexandra James

Playtesters

Brian Aderson, Chris Brann, Mark Denham, Pete Fenner, Dave Laithwait and Ian Roberts

Introduction

The heroes arrive at the hillfort settlement of Anminster. Abandoned more than a thousand years ago, Anminster was built upon the mound of an ancient Dwarven cairn fort. The fort originally consisted of a surface stone tower, overlooking the lands around, but was built downward into the artificial motte in three levels. Beneath the fort was a cairn for the honoured dead, extending another level deeper; beneath that cairn was the true purpose for the fortress: the tomb wherein the phylactery of the Lich Kelamaz lies imprisoned.

After a thousand years of imprisonment under Dwarven seals meant to keep his power contained, the seals blessed by Dwarven Ancestor-Priests have weakened and Kelamaz is slowly reforming in his tomb. Reaching out, he has already reanimated the Dwarven remains beneath Anminster and is seeking to raise the dead in the cemetery above. If left unchecked, his power will grow until he is released and can reign again. Unless the Dwarven seals keeping Kelamaz imprisoned are reinforced by artefacts still lying in the cairn below Anminster, the realm will likely fall once again under his evil spell.

Key Non-Player Characters

- Kelamaz the Lich: Imprisoned undead necromancer entombed beneath Anminster Keep.

- Jared Anminster: Lord of Anminster, fourth generation descendent of the founder. Never much of an outdoorsman, Jared prefers his books and home comforts.

- Sergeant Daymond Yarnek: Lord Anminster's acting Warden and commander of the fort's militia. Resides at Anminster Keep and heartily disapproves of Lord Jared's timidity.

- Relgan Lothbeer: Dwarven proprietor of The Slaughtered Ettin. The stout and loud landlord is well-renowned for his tall stories of adventures from his famed "early days" as an adventurer.

Key Adventure Points

1. The adventurers arrive at Anminster and uncover news of banditry on the nearby causeway.

2. Anminster's dead rise from the grave and the adventurers must help defend the village.

3. Hearing noises beneath his Keep, Lord Anminster summons the adventurers to his aid.

4. The adventurers enter the forgotten Dwarven Underfort and discover the truth about Kelamaz.

5. The players stop Kelamaz's escape, or they die trying.

Timeline of Kelamaz's Escape

The adventurers arrive in Anminster, triggering the breaking of the first seal binding Kelamaz. The Lich has already raised all the uninterred dead in the Dwarven Cairn beneath Anminster.

Start the clock at nightfall on the day the adventurers arrive. Each new day's events begin at nightfall.

Day Two

The second seal is broken. Kelamaz raises the dead in Anminster graveyard, causing an attack on the inn and stables. Inhabitants of the Keep hear tapping in the tower.

In the morning, Lord Anminster summons the adventurers to investigate the tapping in the tower. The adventurers discover the Dwarven Underfort.

Day Three

The third seal is broken. Dead humanoids within 20 kilometres (12 miles) of Anminster automatically rise as Zombies within 24 hours of their death.

Party Size

This module assumes a party of three to five adventurers. If the party is of a different size, the Games Master will need to adjust the encounters as appropriate. In the spirit of Classic Fantasy, it's suggested that you leave things as they are in early encounters to allow you to judge the player's progress. Adding or subtracting one skeleton per two characters is a good starting point with each undead encounter.

Day Four:

The fourth seal is broken. A huge and terrifying thunder storm forms above Anminster, lashing the Tor with rain. Animals within the village are driven mad with fear. Humanoids within the village make a Willpower Resistance roll or flee as per the effects of a Magnitude 12 Fear spell.

Day Five

The final seal is broken. Kelamaz leaves the tomb that holds him. He uses Dimension Door to travel to the surface, arriving on the top of the tower at Anminster Keep. From there, he wages war on the inhabitants.

Areas Covered

The adventurers may choose to visit several locations that are of special significance to this adventure:

- The Slaughtered Ettin Inn: a popular and lively inn located just outside Anminster's east gate.

- The Ettinmarsh Causeway: the ancient trackway which crosses Ettinmarsh and allows trade north to south.

- Anminster Keep: the fortified manor house of Lord Anminster.

- Dwarven Cairns: the tombs built to contain Kelamaz beneath the Underfort.

Kelamaz the Wizard

Around 1300 years ago, an Elven wizard of great power named Kelamaz built Moonspike Tower. He was reclusive and absorbed in his work, seeking to construct a magical portal that could link with the other ancient Moongates that can be found dotted across the lands. Kelamaz built an impressive arch at the top of his tower and wrestled with the conundrum for decades. Eventually, Kelamaz is believed to have stepped through his portal and disappeared for 13 years. When he returned, Kelamaz was transformed into a Lich.

The Coming of the Dragon Kings

The Dragon Kings first conquered Mystamyr 1200 years ago. Arriving from the southwest, their armies of Dragonmen marched first to conquer the city of Zorastor. The Dragon Kings ordered a causeway built across the marshland surrounding Moonspike Tower and their Dwarven thralls succeeded in building it. As the first wagons rolled north from Zorastor, however, there arose from the marshes animated skeletons who slew the waggoneers. Once the goods failed to arrive, Dragon Knights from Kelethin rode south to investigate and were themselves attacked by foul undead. They discovered the zombie forms of the waggoneers among their attackers. Word spread about the awakening of Kelamaz the Lich.

The Defeat of Kelamaz

The Dragon Kings ordered the Dwarves of Zirazund to raze Moonspike Tower. Marching south, the Dwarven Lord camped upon the hill north of the lake. Wasting little time, the Dwarves built boats and crossed directly to the tower. On the shores of Lake Mirrormere they were met by a silent army of skeletal warriors who fought in eerie silence. Defeating these creatures, the remaining Dwarven soldiers approached Moonspike Tower and confronted Kelamaz.

The ancient wizard was an Elf no more: his flesh was gone and his robes contained a skeletal form which blazed with necromantic energies. Only their natural resistance to magic saved the Dwarves from his enchantments and battle was joined. For forty days and forty nights the Dwarves besieged Moonspike Tower. At the end, toppled from the peak of his tower, Kelamaz fell. To this day, none can say why he did not use his portal to escape.

Within the tower the Dwarves discovered a mysterious adamantine jar which glowed with energy and could not be damaged by mortal weaponry or shattered by the spells of the Ancestor-Priests – the phylactery of Kelamaz. Fearing the necromancer's return, the Dwarven Lord interred the phylactery in a cairn upon the hill opposite Moonspike Tower. Every item from the wizard's laboratory was either destroyed or removed and interred with Kelamaz's remains; the Dwarves placed wards around the cairn and sealed the tomb entrance. Upon this place, they built a second cairn within which they interred their honoured dead – all who had died in the battle of Moonspike Tower – as a symbol of their ultimate victory. Finally, a watchtower was built above the cairn to protect the bones of the warriors and maintain a vigil over Kelamaz.

For 800 years, the Dwarves kept guard until they joined the Great Alliance against the Dragon Kings. During that war the Dragonmen marched across the causeway and besieged the Dwarven watchtower, razing it to the ground. From this time forward, the Dwarves withdrew to Zirazund and the lands around Moonspike Tower fell into disuse.

The Founding of Anminster

Anminster was founded by Lord Eadmund Anminster four generations ago. He was given permission by the King to build a watchtower to guard the causeway across Ettinmarsh. Finding the ruins of a round tower at the peak of a hill overlooking the nearby lake, Lord Anminster rebuilt it and used it as the foundation for his own Keep. The village grew up naturally around the Keep, as traders along the Old North Road began to stop to rest before the long trek across the causeway. As Lord Anminster increased his household guard, the village also became a fort and haven for adventurous folk. Even the barbarian tribes inhabiting the grass plains north of Anminster saw the value of the stronghold and began trading hides with the locals instead of raiding.

The Shadow of Moonspike Tower

Although the villagers always stayed away from the Ettinmarsh, fearing rumours of fell creatures in the shadow of Moonspike Tower, some enterprising trappers recently began to poach on the far side of Lake Mirrormere. Having encountered little resistance, the locals have become emboldened and strayed close to the ancient ruined tower itself. Fearing the humans, the Ettin who lives there raised his concerns to the Ettinmoot at last year's meeting and sought to recruit some protection. A local Goblin tribe, seeing the dry accommodations and the value of an Ettin ally, have moved into Moonspike Tower.

Being much closer to the causeway has tempted the Goblin's leader to conduct raids on some of the wagons passing between Zorastor and Sharna. After the first raid, about two weeks ago, Lord Anminster ordered his garrison to investigate the source of the Goblins. The Warden, Janus Elias, decided to lead a group of twelve men into the Ettinmarsh following the tracks left by the Goblins; he tracked them almost to Moonspike Tower. Before anyone could report back to Anminster, however, the Goblins attacked the Warden's men and all perished in the marshes. Since then the guardsmen at the village have been ordered not to patrol the causeway road. Now the Goblins can raid freely and it seems that nobody is prepared to stop them. Trade along the road is dwindling.

Secrets in Anminster

When Eadmund Anminster rebuilt the Dwarven watchtower it was the only visible element of the fort above ground. He hired a Dwarven architect but chose to keep knowledge of the fort beneath a secret. This knowledge was passed to his son, Geoffrey Anminster. Geoffrey's children, however, did not learn of the secret before he perished in battle against the Ettins during the Ettinstrife War. Jared has, however, uncovered an old note, hidden inside an ornate chest wherein old records were kept. The note is addressed to Geoffrey and details the location of the secret entryway to the fort below. Jared Anminster is ready to consider opening the old Dwarven ruins but fears doing so will defile the place and earn the ire of forgotten Dwarven spirits.

NPCs & Luck Points

Unlike standard Mythras, in Classic Fantasy it is not unusual for non-player characters important to the story to possess Luck Points in the same way as a player character. This also applies to non-player character's possessing a character class such as a fighter, cleric, thief, etc. Encounters involving opponents with their own Luck Points will typically play out as a war of attrition, with both sides wearing out the other until one finds themselves 'out of luck'. This will typically eliminate an anticlimactic ending, and allow a lone opponent of importance a little more longevity when outnumbered by a full party of adventurers. These Luck Points work in the same way as those of a player character, granting the same possibilities. The one caveat however is that a non-player character's Luck Points do not regenerate from session to session, instead lasting the length of the adventure. Only by escaping their fate and surviving to take part in another adventure will their Luck Points return. Therefore, it is not unusual for intelligent non-player characters to use their remaining Luck Points in an attempt to flee an impending demise, possibly going on to become a reoccurring villain.

Involving the Adventurers

There are lots of ways to get the adventurers involved in the story. Here are a few suggestions:

1. The adventurers hear from a travelling merchant that the Old North Road, betwixt Zorastor and Sharna, is being plagued with bandits at the causeway near the village of Anminster. The Lord has set a bounty upon the bandits and seeks brave souls to rid him of this menace. Now at the village, strange events begin to unfold…

2. The adventurers are hired by a wealthy patron in either Zorastor or Sharna to locate a trade caravan that is several days overdue. Travelling to Anminster, they hear of the local troubles and investigate further…

3. A Cleric or Druid receives a dream or vision revealing a brooding evil arising at Anminster. They see the Tor, next to the lake and surrounded by marshlands, being engulfed in darkness and feel compelled to go and intervene…

4. A Thief in the party receives word from Gangle (see page 12) that he needs help with a problem in Anminster. Valuable guild traffic is being disrupted by raids on wagons travelling between Zorastor and Sharna. The guild master needs an agent to investigate and resolve the problem…

Rumours

Have each player roll 1d10 and award their character with some rumoured lore. Note that true rumours are marked with (T), half-truth with (1/2T) and false ones with (F).

RUMOUR TABLE

1d10	Rumour has it that…
1	An Elven wizard of great power built Moonspike Tower, more than 1000 years ago. (T)
2	Geoffrey Anminster, grandfather of the current Lord, perished in battle during the Ettinstrife War around 70 years ago. (T)
3	Anminster Tor is cursed and the Dwarves refused to help Lord Anminster build his Keep there. (F)
4	Master Peregrine's horses are of high quality and his prices are the best in all Mystamyr. (T)
5	The mad boatman, Zephaniah Lucerne, built ships for the Dragon Kings and has lived in Anminster longer than anyone else due to his half-elven blood. (F)
6	Moonspike Tower was sacked by the Dwarves during the reign of the Dragon Kings, but the building itself proved immune to fire and catapult. (1/2T)
7	Anminster's Warden and all his soldiers went missing in the Ettinmarsh while searching for bandits. (T)
8	On a misty day, skeletal warriors can be seen standing on the shores of Lake Mirrormere opposite the village. (F)
9	Lake Mirrormere is cursed and those who stray too far from Anminster never return. (1/2T)
10	Trade between Zorastor and Sharna has never been good because Anminster sits next to a huge marsh that wagons can't traverse. (F)

Anminster Village

Read to the Players...

Anminster Tor, the steep hill upon which the fort sits, rises from the marshlands and is crowned by a wooden stockade. The stockade walls stand 10 metres (30 feet) tall, with the circular stone tower that marks the Keep rising even higher. A dozen or more smoke trails rise from within, evidence of chimneys that you cannot yet see. As you come closer, following the track that approaches from the east, you see the tall wooden watch towers and the gate between. Before the gates stand three buildings: a tall and imposing structure on the left from which can be heard music and loud voices; to the right is a stable, adjacent to a fenced horse paddock, and a nearby large wooden house. Guards can be seen on the towers, spears glinting some 15 metres (50 feet) above the steep rise of the hill in front of you. The slope looks gentler on this side, with the trackway rising straight towards the waiting gate.

About the Village

Type: Fortified Manor / Village

Population: 125

Government: Feudal Lord, Anminster Family

Reaction to Outsiders: Suspicious but welcoming.

Economic Outlook: Fair; main trading point on the Old North Road between Sharna and Zorastor.

Prices & Taxes: High prices for many goods; local taxes are fair.

Settlement Issues: Goblin bandits; falling trade traffic.

Threats: Kelamaz the Lich; The Moonspike Goblins.

The fort of Anminster sits atop Anminster Tor, a steep hill on the northern shore of Lake Mirrormere; the fort is some three miles west of the causeway road that runs southwards through the Ettinmarsh. From the vantage of the 15 metre (50 foot) high walls of Anminster Keep (itself 15 metre (50 feet) above the marshlands between the Tor and the road), the guards can see the horizon at about 20 kilometres (12 miles) away.

The Keep is the higher of the two sections of the fort, surrounded by a 6 metre (20 foot) high wooden stockade with a 1.5 metre (five foot) wide walkway around most of its curving circumference. The major feature is the 15 metre (50 foot) high round tower that was constructed upon the ruins of an older Dwarven stone structure; one can plainly see the changing colour and style of stone between the first and second floors. On the northern side of the tower rises the rectangular stone manor house. The upper walls are crenelated and feature a 6 metre (20 foot) wide area behind which rises the steep roof of the main building. In the small yard below stands a large barn and stable for the Lord's horses.

The lower bailey stands three metres (10 feet) lower than the Keep, wooden stockade walls of similar design arcing between pairs of sturdy wooden watch towers at the western and eastern ends of the village. Through the heart of the settlement between the gates runs a wide road of packed earth. Almost two dozen buildings lie within the walls of Anminster village.

Most of the buildings in Anminster are one of two basic designs: most common is the wooden 12 metre (40 foot) long and 6 metre (20 foot) wide structure that is formed of two sections, usually split between a living space and a workshop space; the other design is a 6 metre (20 foot) square wooden building used as a simple house.

Lord Anminster expects trained militia to protect the village but also employs a remnant of 12 professional foot soldiers for full-time duty (the other 12 went missing in the Ettinmarsh two weeks ago, while fighting bandits). Two of these soldiers are assigned to each of the four watchtowers, while four more soldiers serve at the Keep. There is a gate toll of one copper penny per head for non-residents entering Anminster, but the guards enjoy charging two to five copper pennies and pocketing the difference.

Anminster & Environs

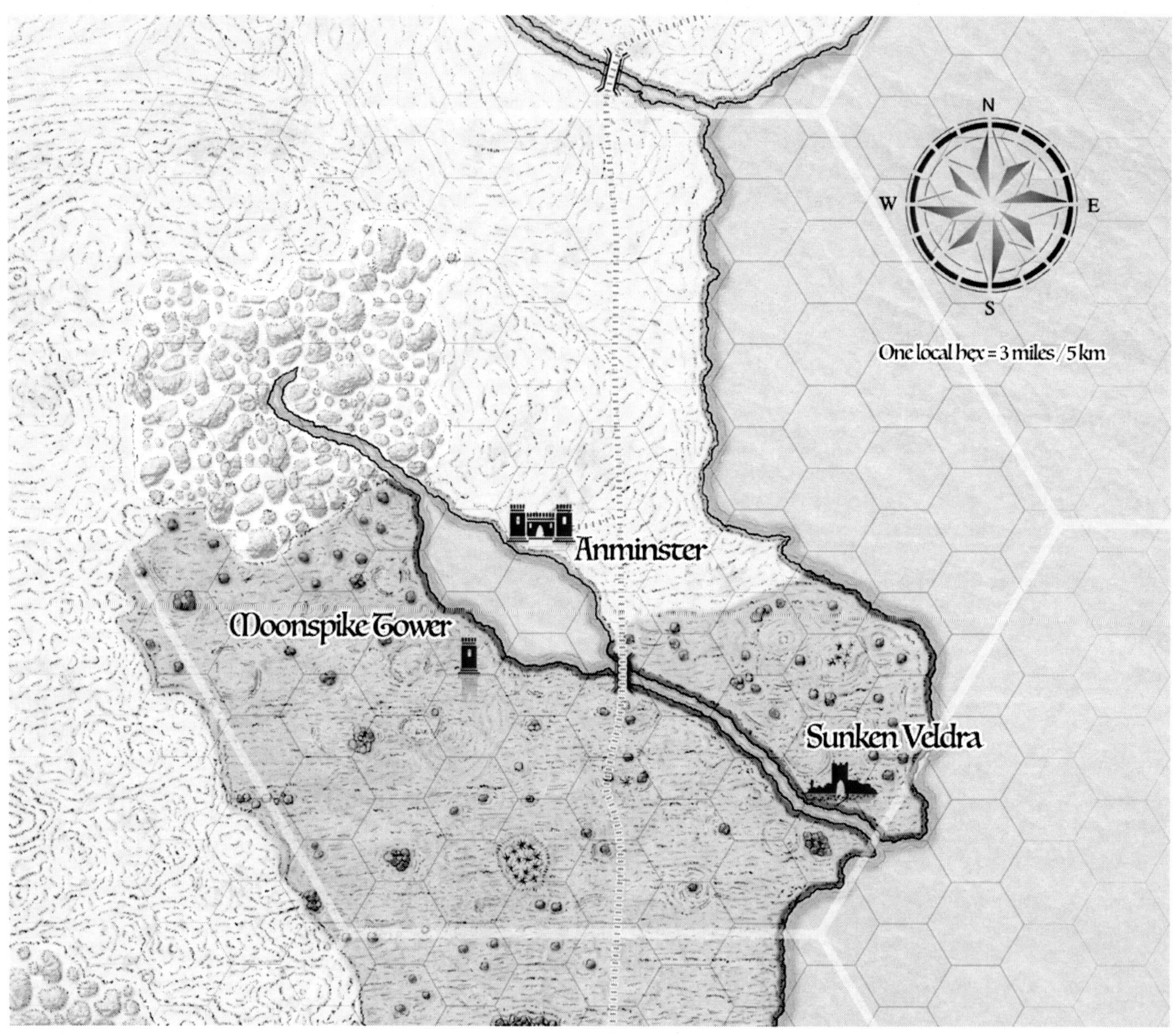

Anminster Village

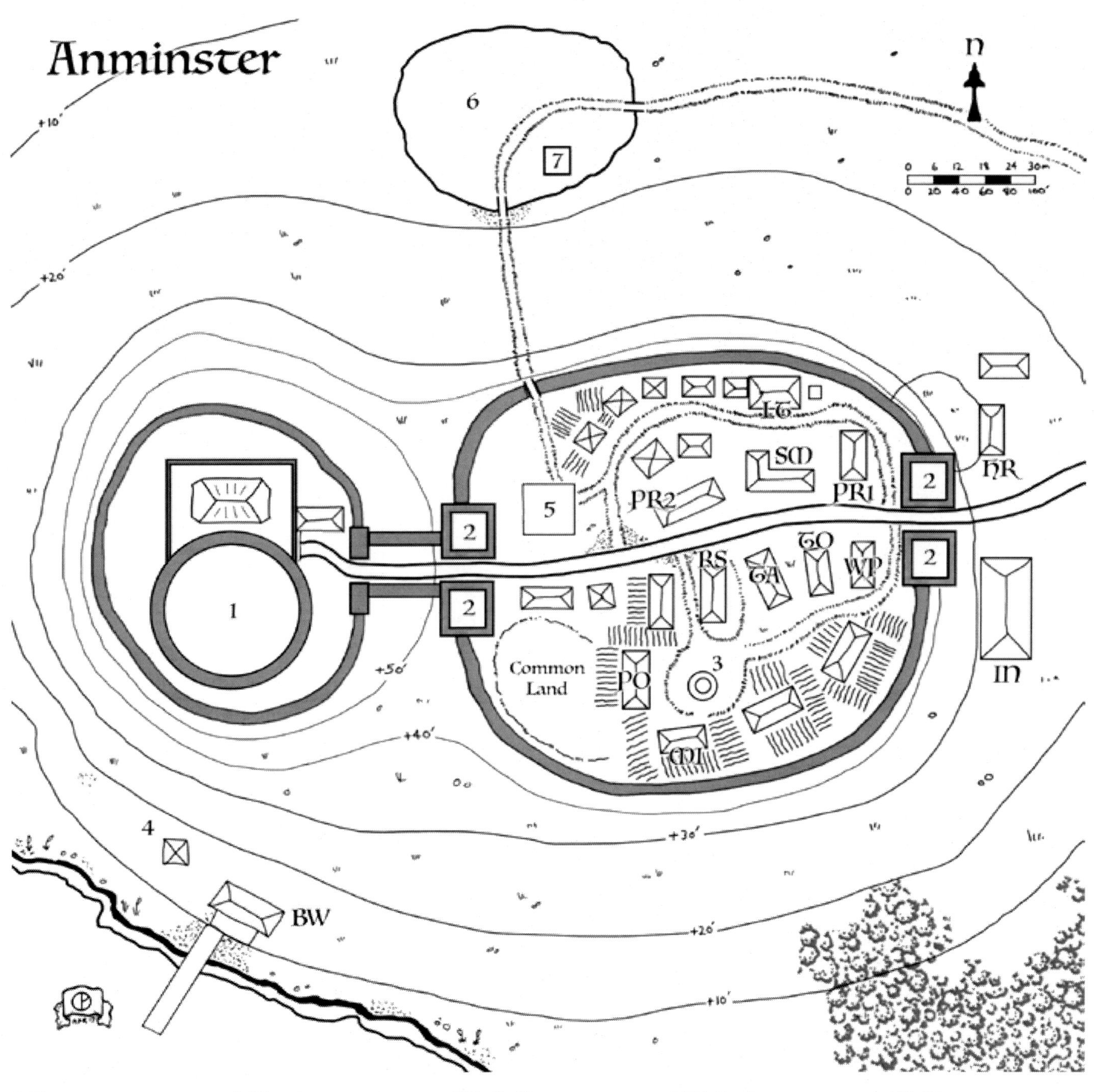

1: Keep	5: Temple	HR: Stables	PR1: Equippery	TA: Toggery
2: Watchtowers	6: Cemetery	LT: Oxhead & Goatskin	PR2: Olwyn's Foods	TO: Tool Shop
3: Well	7: Mausoleum	MI: Melweather's	RS: Gangle's	WP: Hammer & Blade
4: Shrine	BW: Boathouse	PO: Ma Rhonda's	SM: Forge	IN: Inn (The Slaughtered Ettin)

Anminster Keep (1)

The Keep is fully detailed in a later section. See page 15 for further information.

Watchtowers (2)

Each of the watchtowers is 15 metres (50 feet) tall and constructed from wooden logs. There is a platform at the top of each 12 metre (40 foot) square tower from which guards look out over the surrounding countryside. At a total height of 27 metres (90 feet) above the surrounding countryside, watchers at the top of each tower can see approximately 20 kilometres (12 miles). The only blind spot is towards the west, which rises three metres (10 feet) higher than the main village hilltop; soldiers on the roof of Anminster Keep's tower predominately watch westwards.

Each watchtower has five floors:

- The ground floor dedicated to the gate guards, dealing with toll collection.

- The second floor is a dedicated armoury, holding stores of spare spears and shields.

- The third and fourth floors provide sleeping quarters and common storage spaces for guards on duty.

- The fifth "floor" is the crenelated roof.

A typical duty watch consists of four guards: two on the ground floor and two on the tower roof; an additional two guards are expected to be on standby and quarter in the tower. The southern watchtower in each pair is equipped with an alarm bell on a pole that can be hand-rung. Since losing half the guard to the bandits, the duty watch no longer patrols the stockade at night. One guard walks between the towers at half-hour intervals during the day, reducing the tower roof to one guard. No lights are maintained on the stockade wall at night, although a brazier on each tower sheds dim light around the tower for 12 metres (40 feet).

Between each pair of watchtowers stands a gateway. This forms part of the palisade, a 6 metre (20 foot) high wooden stockade, and features a pair of thick wooden gates. The left-hand gate also has a wicket (small door) to allow access when the main gates are closed at night. Residents using the east gate's wicket pay a single copper coin to re-enter Anminster after visiting the inn, while strangers are turned away.

There are a few standard bounties that Sergeant Yarnek is authorised to offer:

- Bandits – five silver pieces per head.

- Ettin – one gold piece per pair of heads.

- Rescue/return of residents – one gold piece per person.

Well (3)

Near the centre of Anminster there is a stone well which is about three metres (10 feet) in diameter and one metre (3 feet) high. There is a wooden frame rising above the hole which is covered with a sloping roof. Running from a crank handle attached to the frame is a rope and bucket which can be lowered 14 metres (45 feet) down to the water below. The locals use the well daily, although visitors are discouraged from watering animals from this source. Locals claim that the well is older than the village. Close examination of the well's stonework will reveal Dwarven stone mason markings that confirm the structure's origin as "the 17th year during the reign of the Dragon Kings".

Shrine to the Lady (4)

On the southern slope of Anminster Tor, not far from the boathouse, stands a small shrine. The southern side of the shrine, facing the lake, is open to the elements. A statue of the Lady Nimue stands inside the shrine. She faces the lake with one hand upraised and the other with the palm horizontal to the ground. The other three walls of the shrine are made of stone and bear runes which are like those used by the tribesmen who trade at Anminster. These runes list the many names of the Lady and there are some 300 different names in all. Locals believe that the shrine stands to remind all that the Lady is keeping watch over Ettinmarsh so that no evil would ever dare cross the lake.

Temple of the Ten Thousand (5)

The Temple of the Ten Thousand stands in Anminster as a tribute to all known and accepted deities. Inside the stone walls of the temple, itself a colonnaded square, are thousands of small shrines. Most of the shrines feature the small statue of a deity around which offerings are left by the faithful. There is no formal priesthood at the Temple but there are two servants who tend to the shrines daily, paid for by the coins and other offerings dropped in a large central collection bowl. Sometimes villagers donate offerings of food or drink for the Temple servants from their own bounty. The names of the servants are Reiniger and Diener.

Walled Cemetery (6)

Outside the north wall of Anminster, on the slopes near the postern gate, stands a gated low stone wall. The roughly oval-shaped area is a cemetery. Families have small plots allocated to them and pay for the upkeep of their ancestor's gravestones, with richer families being located higher up the slope. The most prominent feature of the graveyard is the large mausoleum (detailed below), but there are many other impressive monuments. Funeral processions usually begin at the family home before moving to the Temple of the Ten Thousand for ritual mourning, and then on to the cemetery for cremation or burial.

Anminster Mausoleum (7)

The Anminster family is interred within the 6 metre (20 foot) square mausoleum that stands at the highest point of the cemetery. There are a single pair of iron doors on the northern side of the structure to allow entry, although these doors have no visible handles. Inside lie the remains of three generations of the Anminster family: Eadmund, Geoffrey, and Felton Anminster. Alongside these patriarchs lie their wives and most favoured servants. The patron deity of the family is The Lady, and tributes to her decorate the outside walls. The crest of the Anminster family is carved into the iron doors.

Zephaniah's Boathouse (BW)

Shop Type: Boatwright

Interior: Ratty

Stock Depth: Above Average

Prices (% of standard): 150%

Attitude: Humble

People: Master Zephaniah.

Zephaniah Lucerne is a reclusive and somewhat odd fellow. He's a boat maker renowned for his innovative designs. The eastern end of his home functions as a four metre (15 foot) wide house and the rest is the boathouse proper. A narrow wooden pier extends from a three metre (10 foot) wide platform in front of the boathouse, extending 10 metres (30 feet) out into the lake. Moored at the pier are 7 small fishing boats used by villagers and maintained by Zephaniah. Near the section of the pier on the slope stands a part-built two-metre-long (7 foot) boat which the craftsman is constructing. The boathouse has space to store the fishing boats and Zephaniah charges both mooring and storage fees to the locals.

Master Peregrine's Stables (HR)

Shop Type: Horses

Interior: Shiny

Stock Depth: Above Average

Prices (% of standard): 75%

Attitude: Poker-faced

People: Master Anfel, Katlin (wife), two sons, one daughter.

The stables feature two buildings and an enclosed pasture used to graze horses under Master Anfel Peregrine's care. There is a chest-high wooden fence surrounding the enclosure within which several horses and ponies are grazed. Forming part of the perimeter is a wooden stable with an attached barn; the structure is two-storied with a hay loft. Nearby stands Anfel's residence and workshop, another wooden building of similar proportions. Inside the stable, adventurers will be struck by the immaculate standards of cleanliness and many glittering trophies from a variety of agricultural shows. The master has two journeymen, Besan and Iafor, and his sons work as stable hands too. His animals are renowned for their good quality and his prices are perhaps the best in all Mystamyr.

Oxhide and Goatskin (LT)

Shop Type: Leathercrafter

Interior: Modest

Stock Depth: Below Average

Prices (% of standard): 150%

Attitude: Polite

People: Master Amos, Ella (wife), two sons.

This shop is a wooden building, with the eastern end forming the home of the proprietor and his family, while the western end is the workshop and shop floor. At the west side is another square building that forms a tannery. When hides are being cured, you can smell Master Amos' wares across most of the village. Aside from the smell of the tannery, however, the shop is clean and the stock well presented. Amos makes good quality clothing and other leather items, including suits of leather armour. One local speciality are his wife Ella's leather boots which are favoured by most villagers, making Oxhide and Goatskin a cobbler's shop too.

Melweather's Magical Wonders (MI)

Shop Type: Purveyor of Magical Wonders

Interior: Brightly decorated

Stock Depth: Below average

Prices (% of standard): 100%

Attitude: Helpful

People: Master Garek, Ilina (wife), Galena (daughter).

Garek Melweather is a specialist purveyor of magical items and other wonders. The family uses the western end of the structure as a house. The shop itself is colourful, with blue and white banners lining the interior walls in vertical strips. There is a large counter towards the rear of the shop, and trestle tables covered in interesting artefacts line the walls. The central space is open and feels airy, although there is a mannequin wearing an impressive suit of silvery armour in the centre of the room.

The armour on the mannequin is a full set of Elven Chain that is Garek's pride and joy. His price is 3,360gp but he might be haggled down to 3,000gp. Aside from this, Garek has Rank 1 magic items but does not deal in potions (leaving this to Ma Rhonda, next door). If the adventurers are searching for something specific, there is a 20% chance of Garek having it if the item is listed on the Miscellaneous Items table (Classic Fantasy, page 270). Garek will purchase magic items from the adventurers at between 30% and 50% of their usual value.

Ma Rhonda's Efficacious Brews (PO)

Shop Type: *Potions*

Interior: *Plain*

Stock Depth: *Thin*

Prices (% of standard): *125%*

Attitude: *Dispassionate*

People: *Ma Rho, Elathar (husband).*

Ma Rho's is a speciality shop providing a range of potions and elixirs. Rho is an Elven woman of prodigious age who lives with her husband. The shop is at the northern end of the building. It has many shelved racks around the walls and a workbench in the centre of the room, covered in bubbling pots and other items of chemical utility, at which Ma Rho sits. Each potion is bottled in a small glass phial with a simple handwritten label to identify the bright-coloured liquid within.

The most common item in the shop is a Healing Balm, named 'Ma Rho's Efficacious Salve'. She sells this for 62sp. Every one of the Type 2 potions, oils, and elixirs (Classic Fantasy, page 284) is available, but only 1d2 phials of each can be bought immediately. If players want a resupply of a favourite potion, oil, or elixir then they must wait 2d6 days for Ma Rho to brew it. Type 3 items can be provided 5% of the time, but Ma Rho cannot brew them if they are not already in the shop. She does not sell Holy or Unholy Water.

Anminster Equippery (PR1)

Shop Type: *Provisioner*

Interior: *Bright*

Stock Depth: *Sparse*

Prices (% of standard): *150%*

Attitude: *Pushy*

People: *Joren, Sera (wife), three sons, two daughters.*

Sera made Anminster Equippery a success; her husband, Joren, is a foppish fool who helps her sell the goods they import from both Zorastor and Sharna. Business has been hit hard by recent events, namely the attack on the Warden and his men. Adventurers who visit this shop are likely to receive a hero's welcome if this pair discover they intend to deal with the Goblin problem.

The shop is bright and airy but the shelves and trestle tables are nearly empty. The shop stocks basic adventuring equipment from the Tools Table (Classic Fantasy, pages 75-76) plus ranged weapon ammunition; exceptions would include specialist tools, which are sold at Tymm's shop opposite. Adventurers will find what they need 15% of the time, but only 1d2 of single items are available and 2d12 of items such as arrows or crossbow bolts.

Olwyn's Food Stuffs (PR2)

Shop Type: *Provisioner*

Interior: *Cramped*

Stock Depth: *Sparse*

Prices (% of standard): *90%*

Attitude: *Stoic*

People: *Olwyn, Peri (wife), five daughters, 1 son.*

Olwyn sells food and other provisions, specialising in trail rations. There isn't much choice but what he sells is of good quality and cheap. Olwyn buys most of the stock from local farmers and is less dependent on traders than many, but he is worried about the fall in business. Peri, his wife, is having an affair with Tymm (across the road) and Olwyn is perhaps the only person in Anminster not to know.

Gangle's Secondhand Emporium (RS)

Shop Type: *Resale Items*

Interior: *Untidy*

Stock Depth: *Above average*

Prices (% of standard): *100%*

Attitude: *Considerate*

People: *Gangle (Dwarf), Quickpaw (Gangle's assistant).*

Gangle buys and sells pretty much anything, providing a resale service to the village. He is also the Guildmaster of Thieves, with authority over any members of the Guild present in the village. Gangle buys items at around 30% of their usual price and resells them for 100% of their value. Although it's unusual for people to sell him magic items, there is a 10% chance of him having a Rank 1 item the adventurers ask for. The shop has a small business front and a large rear workshop where Quickpaw mends or polishes old kit for sale. The shop feels like a jumble sale, with items all over the trestle tables and shelves.

Gangle is a member of the Thieves' Guild and acts as a fence. He buys from adventurers, using trusted caravan masters to shift high-value items out for sale in Zorastor and Sharna. Quickpaw can brew poisons (for a price), allowing Gangle to provide a lucrative service to members of the Black Lotus Assassin's Guild too.

Thief characters are expected to visit Gangle and pay tribute; any jobs done in Anminster require Gangle's approval and are subject to the usual Guild percentages applied to fees paid. Gangle does not tolerate burglary in the village and much prefers illicit trade opportunities. His own business is heartily supported by the movement of small packets of high-value "product" between Zorastor and Sharna; Gangle imports a yellow hallucinogenic powder northward, known in Sharna as "Drift", while sending southward an occasional box packed with ice containing scavenged humanoid organs, such as heart or brain. Few questions are asked.

Iona's Forge (SM)

Shop Type: *General Smith*

Interior: *Modest*

Stock Depth: *Average*

Prices (% of standard): *125%*

Attitude: *Accommodating*

People: *Mistress Iona, Perrin (partner).*

Mistress Iona is a forthright and well-renowned blacksmith who provides most of the horse shoes and other metal items for the village. Tymm commissions tool blades from her and Haldan asks her to repair weapons. Perrin is Iona's assistant who lives in the smaller extension at the rear of the main workshop. The two women are viewed as living in a scandalous relationship by most of the villagers, but their work is too valued to tempt anyone into treating them discourteously.

Evann's Toggery (TA)

Shop Type: *Tailor*

Interior: *Well-appointed*

Stock Depth: *Robust*

Prices (% of standard): *150%*

Attitude: *Charming*

People: *Master Evann, Ivana (wife), 2 sons, 1 daughter.*

Evann is a master tailor and makes fine clothing, most of which is sold to the Lord at a ludicrous mark-up. Aside from good fashion, Evann also makes a range of good-quality common clothing and is renowned for the good styling his wife promotes around the village. Evann makes furs and can provide bespoke tailoring for adventurers. Evann and Ivana are personal friends of Lord Anminster and would happily make an introduction on behalf of the right people.

Tymm's Tool Shop (TO)

Shop Type: *Tools*

Interior: *Neglected*

Stock Depth: *Average*

Prices (% of standard): *100%*

Attitude: *Disinterested*

People: *Tymm, Areadne (sister)*

Tymm is a talented craftsman who makes tools for the village. He purchases blades from Iona's forge and then finishes each with a finely-crafted handle. He is renowned for providing full sets of tools in beautifully made wooden tool boxes. His sister, a widow, lives with him and provides for his home. Tymm is interested in only two things: his work, which is akin to art, and his illicit lover Peri (wife of Olwyn).

Hammer and Blade (WP)

Shop Type: *Weapons*

Interior: *Neat*

Stock Depth: *Average*

Prices (% of standard): *150%*

Attitude: *Overbearing*

People: *Halden, Peoni (wife), Kyle (elder son), Katherine (adult daughter).*

Halden is a trader who stocks assorted weapons and fighting supplies. He buys from traders in Zorastor and has found it harder to get stock due to the Goblin problem. Common weapons are available here, although he does not stock ammunition. He'll send customers to the Anminster Equippery for arrows and crossbow bolts. His daughter, Katherine, is a beautiful unmarried woman; local rumour suggests that she is overly critical of her paramours and there are even whispers that she is cruel in her sexual desires. Adventurers who stop the banditry will receive a 50% discount (making prices 75% of standard).

The Slaughtered Ettin Inn (IN)

Shop Type: *Inn*

Interior: *Spacious*

Stock Depth: *Below Average*

Prices (% of standard): *125%*

Attitude: *Friendly*

People: *Master Relgan, Pieter (Journeyman), two waitresses, Fel (Half-Orc work hand)*

Slaughtered Ettin Bill of Fare

Springmead, the finest beverage from Relgan's cellar: three silvers for an evening's ever-flowing mug.

Fel's Best Ale, frothing with refreshment: one silver per mug for an evening's ever-flowing mug.

Finest Elf Wine, a cup of red: one silver per cup.

Chugging Ale: two coppers per mug.

Twice-Brewed Beer: one copper per mug.

Meat Stew and Best Ale: twelve coppers for a plate and a mug.

Cabbage Soup and Ale: five coppers for a bowl and a mug.

Bread and Cheese with Wine: twelve coppers for a plate and cup.

Rooms available for one or two patrons: five silvers per night.

The tall and imposing log-built form of the local inn stands proudly in front of the main gates of Anminster. A large and colourful sign depicts a Dwarf with a stupendously large great axe gutting a two-headed giant, whose entrails are spilling from the edge of the painting's frame. The building has two stories with a tall pointed roof and thatching. The iron-bounded heavy wooden main door is closed but a sign in the centre reads, "Come in and know us better!"

Relgan Lothbeer is the Dwarven proprietor of The Slaughtered Ettin. The interior is grand and open, with long rectangular tables arranged in rows across the common room. In the centre stands a stone fire pit with a chimney rising between the roof beams. At the far end of the common room is the bar, behind which can be seen a large kitchen alive with cooking flames and bustling activity. A stairway on the left rises steadily upwards to a balcony above the bar where doors can be seen, hinting at sleeping quarters beyond. Music can be heard echoing around with a warm lilting tone, an illusion emanating from a magical lute which plays a variety of Elven tunes.

Above the fire pit, hung on two hooks and held horizontally, is a great axe. This is Relgan's famed "Blood Axe" and features in more than one of his many tall tales. The axe is magical and will glow when evil creatures are nearby. Adventurers with an Evil passion cause the axe blade to glow a deep orange (like a blade heated in a furnace) as soon as they come within 10 metres (30 feet) of it.

The upper rooms are three doubles with two single beds in each. Each room has a small fireplace and separate chimney. The rooms are at the rear of the building, with fixed leaded windows to let in light. The rooms also contain a chair, a table, a lockable chest for storing gear. There is a chamber pot under each bed.

The rear of the inn has a kitchen, visible from the common room, and some personal quarters used by Relgan. There is a trapdoor that leads to the cellar in the kitchen. A water butt collects rainwater and is placed just outside the rear door. As Relgan is the only resident, and his staff live in the village proper, the inn has no quarters for family or staff.

The cellar below has three major chambers: the first is a brewing room; the second a storage area for casks of ale and mead; the third is a storage area for dry stuffs, such as grain and barley. Relgan hangs some meat in the dry storage area from hooks running along the ceiling beams.

Zombies at Anminster

On the evening of the second day, Kelamaz raises the dead in Anminster graveyard. Run encounters with successive waves of the undead, depending on where the adventurers are located. Each encounter includes 1d2+1 skeletons and 1d2 zombies.

Examples of these encounters include:

- Adventurers at the inn become aware of mindless banging on the doors and the patrons quickly panic.

- Shouts from Master Peregrine's stables will rouse adventurers to the defence of the horses and house.

- Undead assault the small postern gate on the north side, near the graveyard.

- Undead will be found wandering all around the hill outside the walls.

- Anyone venturing to the graveyard will meet undead.

Anminster Keep

The stone round-tower and the attached squat stone fortified house stand atop Anminster Tor like brooding giants. Lower than the tower, the crenelated roof of the house overlooks a small yard and a squat wooden stable. The main doors to the house are made from finely carved oak reinforced with iron bandings that have been cast to mimic the swords that adorn the family crest hanging above. The spear tips and helms of several guards can be seen moving along the roof tops of both the tower and the house.

General Notes

Unless otherwise noted, each ceiling in the tower and house is four metres (15 feet) high and vaulted from the corners with ornate stone. The outer walls are three metres (10 feet) thick and built from stone. Lighting is generally bright, with lamps hanging from at least two walls in each location; at night, many rooms are left in darkness (at your discretion). Most interior doors are made of reinforced wooden construction and without locks (6 AP, 30 HP). Unless otherwise mentioned, door locks are Standard difficulty to pick using thieves' tools.

Keep and Tower First Floor

1. The Gates

The two pairs of ornate doors that give access to the house are made from finely carved oak and reinforced with iron bandings (8 AP, 35 HP). Between them is an area designed to cause delay in any assault from the outside. The Lord's Chamberlain, Aspinus Tonge, will have the outer doors opened for visitors with two militiamen standing either side.

2. The Hallway

The gateway opens on an ornately decorated and plush hallway. At the west end of the hall are spiral stairs which run to the rooftop. Paintings showing past Lords of Anminster run along the south wall.

A single militiaman is posted to provide protection when the Lord is on this floor.

3. The Main Stairway

The stairway runs through to the rooftop. Made of stone and wide enough for a single man to fight on the stairwell, the stairs wind upwards clockwise. On the first floor the stairs open to the wide upper corridor; before reaching the roof, there is an iron gate (12AP, 20 HP) two metres (7 feet) up which is kept closed and can be locked. The roof guards have a bad habit of leaving this stair gate unlocked.

4. The Great Hall

This is a large chamber with two fireplaces and two pairs of oaken double doors. In the centre of the north wall stands an ornate oaken throne from which the Lord dispenses justice. The banner of House Anminster looms behind the throne. There is a 6 metre (20 foot) long oaken table running from north to south surrounded by comfortable oaken chairs, used for guests or villagers to seat themselves. The Lord can be found in this chamber on all but Holy Days from the ninth hour through until the midday meal.

5. The Meeting Hall

In the centre of the room runs a set of long oaken tables around which are arranged many stools. The table functions as a dining space and the Lord's chair is placed at the north end. The walls are decorated with the banners of the houses of Anminster and Sharna, as well as with relic arms and armour from earlier dynasties.

6. Kitchens

There are two large fireplaces over which hang bubbling pots and a rotating spit. In the centre of the room are long wooden workbenches, higher than usual tables to facilitate working while standing. The kitchens have a full-time cook and several scullions, working in shifts split between the early morning to midday and the afternoon through to midnight.

7. Stables

This wooden building is divided into two sections: the western end has four stalls for horses, but the Lord only owns one. The eastern end of the stable is used for shoeing and storage. There is a low-ceiling in the eastern section of the stable allowing for a hay loft and wooden ladder to access it. Horses are walked in the yard outside and ridden out through the village.

8. Tower Gate

This is the tower's main access point. These doors stand open during daylight hours but are closed and locked at night.

9. Gate Chamber

This stone chamber's doors stand open during daylight hours but are closed and locked at night. The chamber is otherwise spartan.

10. Drill Hall

There is a circular stairway that pierces through the ceiling in the south. A secret door (Formidable to detect) hides the stairs to the Underfort. The doors to the north are lockable. The guards use this space for drills and weapon practice, with pairs duelling and quads practicing shield discipline.

Kelamaz Rises: On the second day (see the timeline on page 3), starting at nightfall, a pair of Skeleton Shieldguards begin banging on the secret door, raising attention. By morning the Lord orders that guards stand watch. Sergeant Yarnek recommends that Lord Anminster summon the adventurers and hire them to investigate, as Yarnek does not want to commit the already depleted guards to an unknown danger.

11. Ale Store

Rows of barrels on horizontal trestles run along the circumference of the room's outer wall. Along the southern and eastern walls are vertically stored barrels ready to be moved to a trestle as supplies are used. Servants access this room to draw pitchers of ale and mead for consumption elsewhere in the Keep.

12. Dry Store

Dry goods, such as grain and rice, are stored in this chamber. Raised wooden pallets help to keep the goods off the floor and free of moisture. A tabby cat known as "Alfie" is employed to keep the room free from mice and rats, being fed daily by the servants. The cat has a warm bed on a pallet just inside the door.

13. Main Pantry

This chamber holds racks filled with dairy products, such as milk and cheese. Foodstuffs are neatly arranged on tall wooden frames with three layers of shelves.

14. Meat Store

This room is a meat store with rows of hooks suspended from iron poles running north to south between the walls. There are ample carcasses of beef, pork, and venison for many months of fine dining. Piping runs from floor to ceiling in eight places regularly spaced along the curving outer wall and each pipe is cold to touch.

15. General Storeroom

This room is filled with boxes and containers, mostly storing cutlery and sets of plates or glasses for use in the Keep. In here are also found spare candlesticks, tablecloths, and other paraphernalia relating to the kitchen and Great Hall.

16. Wine Store

Along the circumference of the room's outer wall stand wine racks from floor to ceiling. These hold the oldest vintages of both red and white wine. Parallel to those rearmost racks stand slightly curving arcs of additional racks, arranged in rows running across the width of the room.

17. The Secret Stair

The stone stairway descends to the Dwarven Underfort. The stairway is three metres (10 feet) wide and spirals down in an anti-clockwise direction. There is a secret door which links the chamber to location 10, obvious to anyone inside this area. A pair of Skeleton Shieldguards attack the adventurers when they open (or break down) the door.

Keep and Tower Second Floor

18. Upper Hallway

This is an ornately decorated and plush hallway. At the west end are spiral stairs. Paintings from the history of Mystamyr run along the south wall, most being scenes from the Dragon King War. A single guard is posted here when the Lord is on this floor.

19. Master Bedroom

Lord Anminster's bedroom has two fireplaces and a large oaken (lockable) doorway. In the centre of the north wall stands an ornate

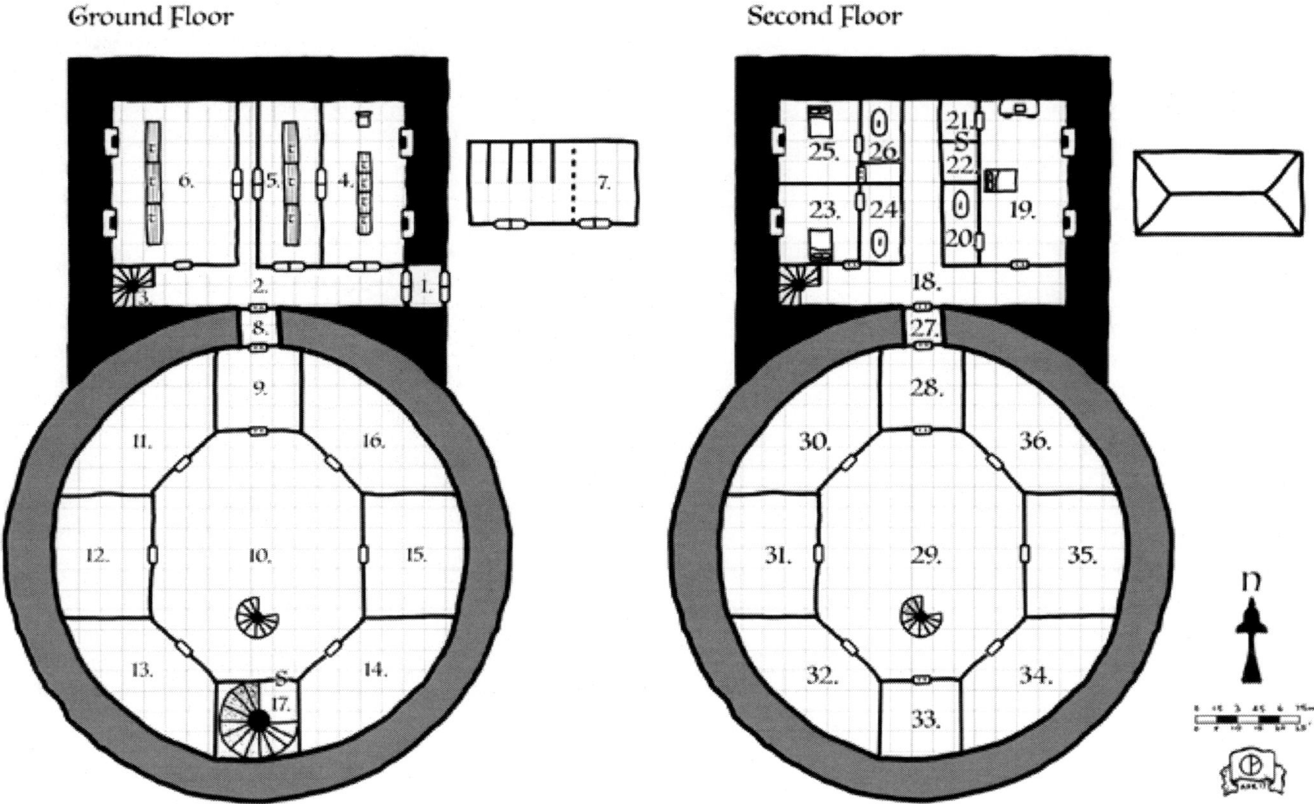

Ground Floor

Second Floor

oaken desk with a plush stool. Next to the desk, on the right, is a wooden chest. The banner of House Anminster hangs above. In the centre of the west wall stands a large four-poster bed with heavy drapes to screen it. The Lord can be found in this chamber from midnight until the ninth hour, sleeping or working at his desk.

Treasure: The desk has a lockable (Hard to pick) drawer on the left-hand side. There is a non-lockable drawer on the right-hand side of the desk. The locked portion of the desk contains private documents and the deeds to the lands around Anminster; there is also a bag containing 120gp and 230sp. The unlocked drawer contains the current ledgers. On the desk are three tomes from the family archive, one of which is open. This reveals the original receipts and work orders for the tower commissioned by Lord Eadmund Anminster. Lying loose on these tomes is a note addressed to Geoffrey Anminster (see below). The chest contains more old ledgers and records from the time of Eadmund Anminster.

> **Dearest Geoffrey,**
>
> **One secret I must entrust to you: there lies below the tower an ancient underfort and, below that, a cairn dedicated to the memory of fallen ancestors. I have built a hidden portal to this ancient ruin but resolved not to open it unless necessity calls. Keep the secret safe. Defile not the memory of that proud race who first laid foundations upon Anminster Tor.**
>
> **Your devoted father, Eadmund**

20. Bathing Chamber

This plain chamber has a stone floor. There is a large ceramic bath near the north end. From a rail on the wall hang a pair of bright blue towels. A large jug suitable for pouring water stands in the north-east corner.

21. Closet

Shelves along the west wall provide space for neatly folded tunics and hose. A rail along the north wall carries several doublets and shirts. On the south wall is a secret door (Hard difficulty Perception test to notice).

22. Safe Room

This chamber is carpeted and contains a small bed, a chamber pot, a backpack filled with 28 days of iron rations, and a large iron chest (12 AP, 60 HP) with a padlock (Hard difficulty to pick). This is used by Lord Anminster as a safe room: should the Keep fall, he will withdraw to this location and await rescue or relief. The chest contains the Lord's personal fortune.

Treasure: 4,000 CP; 2,000 SP; 1,000 GP; 4 Gems (amethyst 100 GP, bloodstone 50 GP, jade 50 GP, blue topaz 10 GP); Gold chalice with four blue topaz gems and a large exquisite tapestry, each worth 100

GP. There is a Bag of Holding (6 ENC, 100 ENC limit), in which all the gold and gems are held.

23. Best Guest Bedroom

The room has a fireplace on the western wall, a bed against the south wall, and plush carpeting. There is an empty wooden chest at the foot of the bed for storing clothing. Under the bed is a chamber pot.

24. Best Guest Bathing Room

This plain chamber has a stone floor. There is a large ceramic bath in the centre of the floor near the south end. From a rail on the wall hang a pair of bright red towels. A large jug suitable for pouring water stands in the south-west corner.

25. Guest Bedroom

The room has a fireplace on the western wall, a bed against the north wall, and plush carpeting. There is an empty wooden chest at the foot of the bed for storing clothing. Under the bed is a chamber pot.

26. Guest Bathing Room

This plain chamber has a stone floor. There is a large ceramic bath near the north end. From a rail on the wall hang a pair of bright yellow towels. A large jug suitable for pouring water stands in the north-east corner.

27. Upper Tower Gates

This forms the tower's secondary access point and is used by servants. These doors stand open during daylight hours and are closed and locked after everyone retires for the night.

28. Upper Gate Chamber

This stone chamber has reinforced wooden doors at the north and south ends. The doors stand open during daylight hours and are closed and locked at night. The chamber is otherwise spartan.

29. Servant's Hall

A circular stairway pierces through both the ceiling and the floor in the southern section of the room. The door to location 33 is a strong iron door with an intricate lock – see that location for details. The doors to the north are lockable. The servants based in Anminster Keep use this space for morning prayers together (an hour before dawn), meetings for all the staff, or for formal inspections.

30. Male Servant's Quarters

This chamber contains a row of beds along the curving outer wall. At the foot of each bed is a small wooden chest for the storage of personal effects, and each person has a chamber pot they are expected to empty each morning. If searched, give each chest a random assortment of coins: 75% chance of 1d4 copper pieces, 50% chance of 1d6 silver pieces.

31. Upper Storage Room

This chamber is reserved as a store for bedding, blankets, pillows, and the other paraphernalia required to service the bedrooms in the main house. There are shelves along the north and south walls.

32. Foul Room

This stone-flagged and chilly room has slots in the outer wall for the disposal of midden, allowing folk to pour out chamber pots. Along the curving wall stand two wooden troughs upon which is placed a wooden seat with an oval hole: a crude toilet. The contents can be emptied manually and poured through the holes in the wall. The room stinks of urine and faeces. The door is kept firmly closed. To mitigate the smell, incense oil is burned in two lamps that hang from the ceiling.

33. Vault

This chamber has a strong iron door (12 AP, 75 HP) with an intricate lock (Formidable difficulty) on the north wall. The interior is lined with a thin 1.25cm (1/2 inch) layer of lead over which painted plaster has been added. The lead is intended to block magical detections and teleportation effects. In the centre of the chamber are three iron boxes about one metre (three feet) long and 60cm (two feet) wide. Each box has a padlock (Hard difficulty), with contents as follows:

Box 1: 11 SP; 10 GP; 3 red jasper gems (50 GP each)

Box 2: 16 GP; jade comb (50 GP), bloodstone necklace (65 GP)

Box 3: 18 SP; 14 GP; 1 pink pearl (100 GP); 1 polished blue coral gem 60 GP, 1 silver-plated steel dagger with a moonstone gem inlaid in the hilt.

34. Servant's Washroom

This chamber is stone-flagged and bare apart from eight water troughs that run along the curving outer wall, each with a wooden pail nearby with which to collect water. Piping from below runs to a tap above each trough, allowing for running cold water. Servants and guards can use this facility to freshen up, although few use it often because cold water washing is not pleasant.

Keep Roof, Tower Third Floor

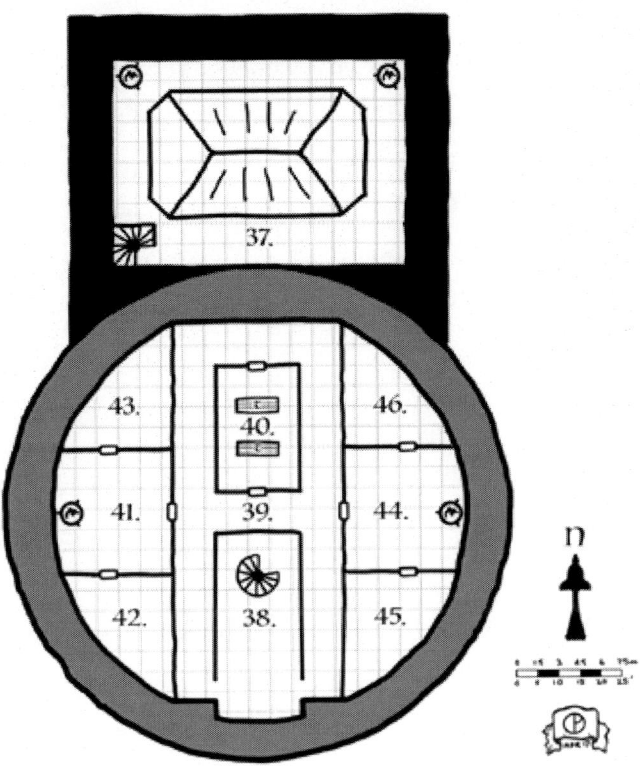

Tower Roof

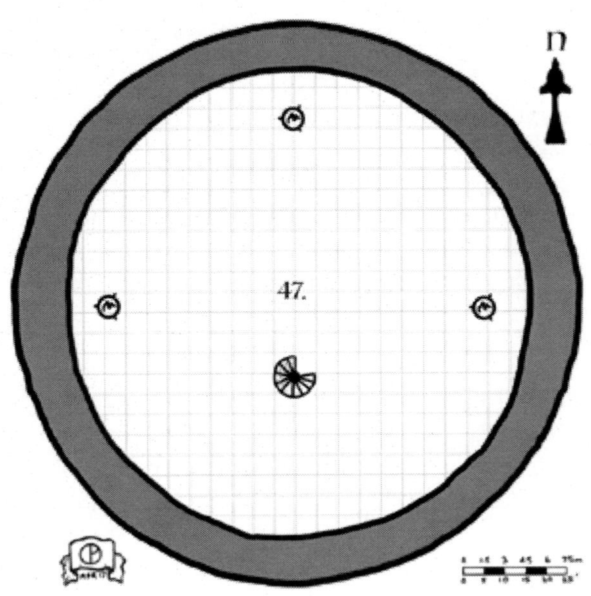

35. Archer's Hall

This chamber has three open arrow slits along the east wall at roughly three metre (10 foot) intervals. The view overlooks the courtyard running down to the inner gates. Barrels of arrows sit in the west corners of the room on either side of the door.

36. Female Servant's Quarters

This chamber contains a row of beds along the curving outer wall. At the foot of each bed is a small wooden chest for personal storage and each person has a chamber pot they are expected to empty. If searched, give each chest a random assortment of small coins: 75% chance of 1d4 copper pieces, 50% chance of 1d6 silver pieces.

Keep Roof, Tower Third Floor and Roof

37. Keep Roof

The top of the keep is crenelated on all sides of the three metre (10 foot) thick outer walls. There is a step up to a 1.5 metre (five foot) parapet on the west, north, and east sides. To the south the tower rises, looming some 6 metres (20 feet) above this level. The south-west corner features the stairway down.

There is an iron gate halfway down the stairs. This gate (12 AP, 20 HP) is supposed to be locked at night but guards frequently leave it unlocked. At each corner of the north wall stand braziers which are lit to provide warmth and light. Two guards patrol both day and night. In the centre, the wooden slats of the main house roof rise to a height of two metres (7 feet), making it hard to see across the area.

38. Stair Room

At the northern end of the chamber a stairway pierces through the floor and ceiling. At this level, the stairs are blocked by an iron gate (12 AP, 20 HP) that is supposed to be kept locked by the soldiers above on the tower roof. The guards frequently leave it unlocked for convenience.

39. Guard Halls

These corridors are designed to be defended should either the roof or lower floors be lost to attackers.

40. Guard Wardroom

Two long benches provide a space for the tower guards to meet and eat together, served from the kitchens far below in the house. In recent weeks, it has fallen into almost complete disuse.

41. Guard Quarters

The room contains eight bunk beds for the guards to use when off duty, arranged along the north and south walls with two beds between each door. A brazier stands near the western outer wall to provide heat and light to the men stationed here. If searched, give each chest a random assortment of small coins: 75% chance of 1d6 silver pieces, 50% chance of 1d4 gold pieces.

42. Armoury

Weapon racks line the east wall containing 14 spears. 12 round shields hang from the curving outer wall. Barrels of arrows sit in the eastern corner (60 arrows total).

43. Guard Store

Shelves line the eastern wall containing supplies of iron rations. A barrel of water sits next to the door. The room is otherwise stacked with boxes and bags of spare kit, such as tunics and blankets, for use by the guards.

44. Guard Quarters

The room contains eight bunk beds for the guards to use when off duty, arranged along the north and south walls with two beds between each door. A brazier stands near the eastern outer wall to provide heat and light. If searched, give each chest a random assortment of small coins: 75% chance of 1d6 silver pieces, 50% chance of 1d4 gold pieces.

45. Guard Store

Shelves line the western wall containing supplies of iron rations. A barrel of water sits next to the door. The room is otherwise stacked with boxes and bags of spare kit, such as tunics and blankets, for use by the guards.

46. Armoury

Weapon racks line the west wall containing 8 spears. 10 round shields hang from the curving outer wall. Barrels of arrows sit in the western corner (48 arrows total).

47. Tower Roof

The top of the tower is crenelated on all sides of the three metre (10 foot) thick outer walls. There is a step up to a 1.5 metre (five foot) parapet on all sides. A circular stairway pierces through the floor near the south side, leading to the second floor. Three braziers stand on the west, north, and east sides. These are lit at night to provide warmth and light to the soldiers on the tower. Two guards patrol both day and night.

The Warrior's Eyrie & Cairns

The Dwarven Underfort named "Warrior's Eyrie" has lain undisturbed for centuries. It stands vigil over the remains of Kelamaz the Lich, although the seals placed to contain that evil are failing. The first three levels of the dungeon are the remains of the Underfort. The fourth level features the cairn within which the Dwarves who fell at the Battle of Moonspike Tower were interred. The adventurers must penetrate to the fifth level wherein lies the Lich's phylactery.

> *Through the hidden doorway, you can see the wide spiral stair which leads downwards into darkness. A fell breeze emanates from the depths and carries the scent of musty rot. You can just make out an eerie clanging sound, as if two metal objects were being hammered upon one another. The dust upon the stairs shows signs of recent disturbance, with claw-like scratches leaving deep marks on the stones.*

The Dwarven Wards

The ancient Dwarves of Zirazund worshipped their ancestors. Their burials involved the Dwarven Ancestor-Priests capturing the life energy of the dead and channelling it into crystals called Soulstones. The life energy could then be communed with by descendants. On occasion, the Ancestor-Priests would find other uses for soulstones.

Because the Dwarves could not destroy Kelamaz's phylactery, it was interred in a tomb warded by five focusing lenses. Each lens is powered by a single soulstone. The lenses focus on a series of magical seals which bind the life energy of Kelamaz into his phylactery. The failure of the seals has been caused by the exhaustion of the energy in each crystal. This has steadily allowed Kelamaz to reach out and manipulate the dead within the Underfort and the village beyond. Even though he cannot escape until all the seals are broken, the Lich is steadily growing in power. It is up to the adventurers to stop him by replacing the exhausted crystals, thus recharging the broken seals.

General Notes:

Each ceiling in the Underfort is four metres (15 feet) high and vaulted from the corners with ornate stone. The outer walls are three metres (10 feet) thick and built from stone. Lighting is generally absent unless otherwise stated. Doors are usually of reinforced wooden construction without locks (AP 6, 30 HP). Some are made from iron (AP 12, 75 HP), as noted in the relevant entries. Unless otherwise mentioned, door locks are all Hard difficulty to pick using thieves' tools. Portcullises are made from iron (12 AP, 10 HP per bar) and can be bypassed if two bars are cut, or if successfully lifted.

Underfort Level 1

1. The Iron Portal

Stairs from the tower above open out into a large chamber. In the centre of the north wall stand a pair of double iron doors engraved with intricate patterns and approached by a 1.5 metre (five foot) tall set of steps. Above the doorway is a lintel stone upon which are engraved Dwarven runes. The walls to the east and west are pierced with five arrow slits spaced at 1.5 metre (five foot) intervals but disguised beneath the imposing form of two extensive floor-to-ceiling murals. The whole space was originally designed to create a killing zone. Evidence of the success of this are patches of brownish-red bloodstaining on the floor where the Dragon King's assaulting soldiers fell; the bodies were later removed and cremated by the victors, leaving only Dwarven remains.

The runes read "Warrior's Eyrie". The designs are consistent with the Houses of Zirazund, bearing their heraldic marks of hammer, helm, and shield. The mural to the west depicts an army of Dwarven warriors surrounding the unmistakable shape of Moonspike Tower. The mural to the east shows a black-robed skeletal figure falling from the pinnacle of the tower onto the remains of a skeletal army, with victorious Dwarves raising their spears in triumph. The iron doors are closed but not locked and open away from the adventurers. These doors are being held shut by the Skeleton Shield-guards on the other side banging with their shields (see location 2).

2. The Battle Hall

From here you can see the whole length of the Battle Hall of which this is the first section. In total, the whole area is 20 metres (65 feet) by 6 metres (20 feet) and pierced by two massive iron portcullises that were dropped in the final defence. The iron doors that once stood in the western and eastern walls each lie on the ground, having been pulled off their hinges during the battle.

Four Skeleton Shieldguards are in this area, pressing against the iron double doors and banging on it with their shields. To push into the room, adventurers will need to succeed at opposed Brawn rolls against these creatures. More skeletons can also be seen up the hall to the north, turning and clamouring to get to the adventurers despite the portcullis stopping them.

2a. The Killing Zone

The centre section of the Battle Hall was designed as a killing zone, with arrow slits every 1.5 metres (five feet) along the east and west walls. The two portcullises block access to the stairs at the far end. The east and west walls are again disguised with full floor-to-ceiling murals. The mural on the west wall depicts a Dwarven funeral parade with dozens of coffins being carried into a barrow on a steep hillside. The mural on the east wall depicts a line of Dwarves in robes carrying a large ornate urn into a circular chamber and placing it upon a raised dais. Six Skeleton Shieldguards are in this area, drawn towards the adventurers but only a threat if they come too close.

2b. The North Stair

The north end of the Battle Hall hosts the North Stair, a stone spiral staircase which goes down to both Level Two (location 9) and Level Three (location 24). Wooden doors give access to the archery galleries either side of the Battle Hall. At the south-west corner, between the door and the portcullis, are two levers and a cranking mechanism to operate the two portcullises dividing the Battle Hall. One Skeleton Shieldguard is in this area, drawn towards the adventurers and banging against the portcullis.

3. The East Stair

The access passageway connects the East Stair to the Battle Hall. The door at the west end has been torn off its hinges and the portcullis halfway down its length has had the three central bars melted. On the floor are countless broken spears, arrows, and shattered shields; all have been burned by an intense fire. The East Stair is a stone spiral staircase which goes down to Level Two (location 9a). Both wooden doors on the north and south sides of the East Stair

have been shattered and leave only empty doorways, again scorched by fire. On the north wall, near the portcullis between here and location 2, is a lever and a cranking mechanism to operate that portcullis. There are scorched skeletal remains, too damaged to have been raised by Kelamaz.

4. The West Stair

The access passageway connects the West Stair to the Battle Hall. The door at the east end has been torn off its hinges but the portcullis halfway down its length is intact. On the floor are countless broken spears, arrows, and shattered shields. The West Stair is a stone spiral staircase which goes down to Level Two (location 9b). Both wooden doors on the north and south sides of the West Stairs have been left ajar. On the north wall, near the portcullis between here and location 2, is a lever and a cranking mechanism to operate that portcullis. There are scorched skeletal remains here.

5. West Armoury

Once used as an armoury, this chamber was stripped by the defenders as they retreated below. The door south is ajar while the door east is closed.

6. West Archer Gallery

This chamber links two archer galleries, allowing the defenders to utilise the arrow slits along the east walls to defend the Underfort. The 1.5 metre (five foot) wide ledge along the east wall is raised 1.5 metres (five feet) above the rest of the room. There is a closed wooden door at the far north-east end. Barrels for arrows sit along the north wall, although these have long lain empty.

6a. West Archer Tunnel

An empty gallery accesses arrow slits along the east wall of this corridor. A barrel containing 2d6 arrows sits at the corner junction.

7. East Armoury

Once used as an armoury, this chamber was stripped by the defenders as they retreated below. The door south is shattered and fire scorched. The door west is wide open.

8. East Archer Gallery

This chamber links two archer galleries, allowing the defenders to utilise the arrow slits along the west walls. The 1.5 metre (five foot) wide ledge along the west wall is raised 1.5 metres (five feet) above the rest of the room. There is a closed wooden door at the far north-west end. Empty barrels for arrows sit along the north wall, one of which is shattered.

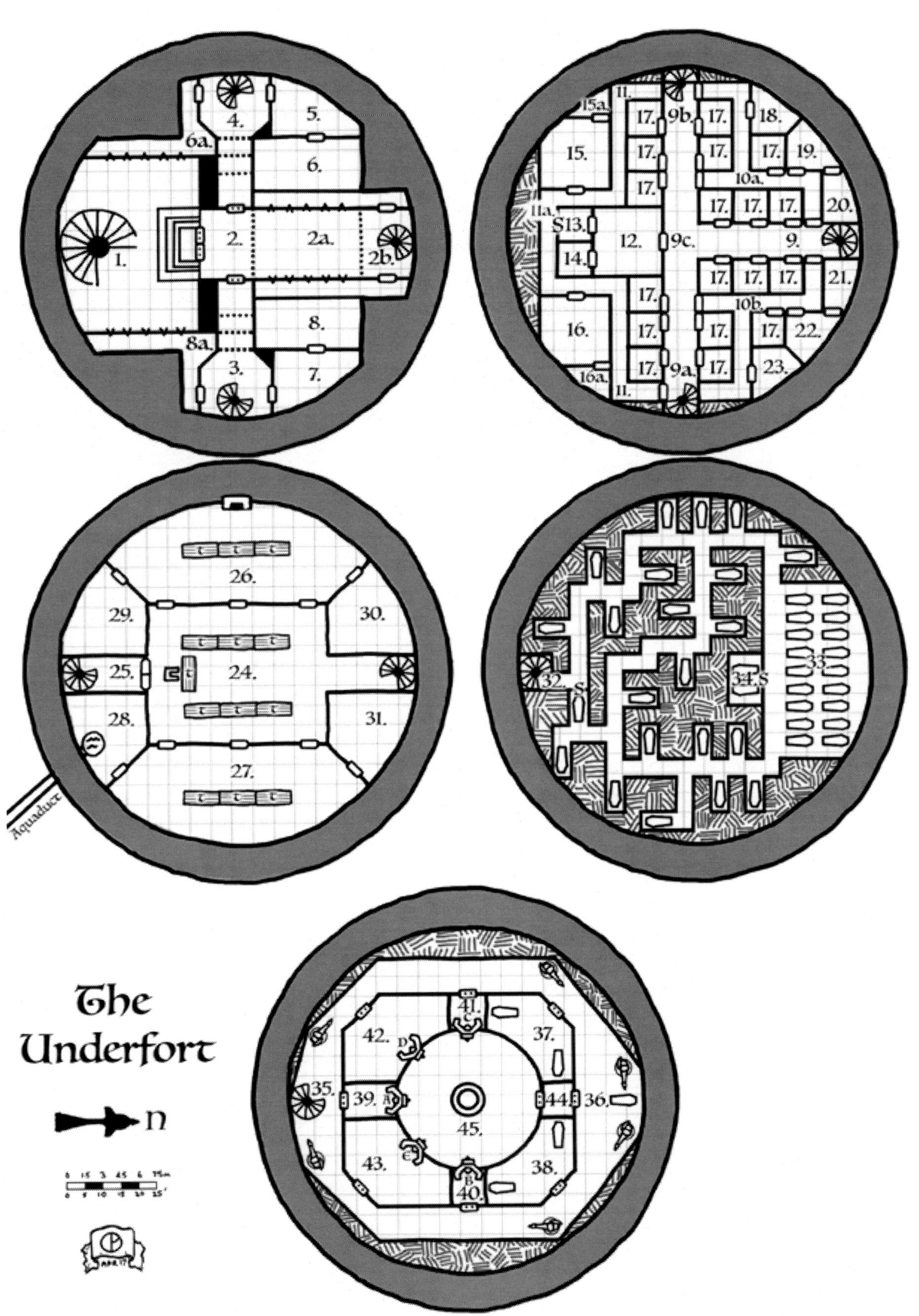
The
Underfort
N
Aquaduct

8a. East Archer Tunnel

An empty gallery accesses arrow slits along the west wall of this corridor. An empty barrel for arrows sits at the corner junction. The door at the north-east end of the tunnels lies shattered in fragments, leaving the portal open and scorched by fire.

Underfort Level 2

This level was designed primarily to garrison the 50 warriors posted to the Eyrie.

9. North Stair Corridor

The north end of the corridor hosts the North Stair, a stone spiral staircase which goes up to Level One (location 2b) and down to Level Three (location 24). Two Skeleton Shieldguards stand as sentries here, facing towards the stairway. Noisy intruders will draw their attention.

9a. East Stair Corridor

The east end of the corridor hosts the East Stair, a stone spiral staircase which goes up to Level One (location 3). Two Skeleton Shieldguards stand as sentries here. They are stationed facing towards the stairway. Noisy intruders will draw their attention.

9b. West Stair Corridor

The west end of the corridor hosts the West Stair, a stone spiral staircase which goes up to Level One (location 4). Two Skeleton Shieldguards stand as sentries here, facing towards the stairway. Noisy intruders will draw their attention.

9c. Main Corridor Intersection

The intersection stands before the closed ornate wooden doors of the Lord's Chamber (location 12). The carvings depict the hammer and wolf's head heraldry of House Kelvan from the Dwarven city of Zirazund. The door is unlocked. Intruders may attract Skeleton Shieldguards at locations 9, 9a, and 9b

10a. Connecting Corridor

This corridor runs to the west side of the complex, connecting several rooms in the north-west quarter.

10b. Connecting Corridor

This corridor runs to the east side of the complex, connecting several rooms in the north-east quarter.

11. Connecting Corridor

This corridor runs to the south side of the complex, connecting several rooms between the east and west sides.

11a. Secret Door

Air flow from the secret door has caused an arc of dust-free stone to form in the corridor. Adventurers who succeed at an easy Perception test will notice this effect. To discover the door, all that is needed is an inspection of the wall. The door is opened by pressing a small piece of stone to the right of the door at about waist height.

12. Lord's Chamber

On entering this room the adventurers will notice the strong scent of pipeweed and see the long-faded glory of the Lord's private bedroom. The oaken bed along the southern wall, between the two doors, has long drapes surrounding it. A moaning and sobbing sound emanates from behind the drapes. Along the west wall stands a desk covered in scattered and faded papers. A large plush chair sits in the north-east corner. On the floor, in front of the bed, is the skeleton of a Dwarf clad in full chain and plate armour with its head missing. The carpet is stained brownish-red with dried blood.

The Haunt: The spirit of Karden Nord remains behind the bed drapes. Adventurers who touch, search, or loot the skeleton attract the ire of the haunt: emerging from the bed, the haunt will scream and invoke its Wither ability. If the adventurers open the drapes and speak to it, the haunt tells them to "Go away!", continuing to sob. See Karden's stats on page 34.

Adventurers persistently communicating with the ghost can learn the following information:

- The ghost is the Dwarven Lord of the Warrior's Eyrie, Karden Nord.

- Karden was killed in this room by the leader of the Dragonmen.

- The Lord was beheaded and his enemy took the head to the Fire Citadel of the Dragon Kings as a trophy.

- To find his rest, Karden's head must be returned to the skeleton.

- Karden will warn the adventurers that "He is breaking free", referring to Kelamaz.

- The ghost will tell the adventurers that to stop Kelamaz they must restore the sacred seals with "the soul gems of the Ancestor-Priests".

Treasure: Karden's skeleton is wearing Plate Mail, +1. This armour is SIZ 11 and covers the Chest, Abdomen, Legs, and Arms. The ghost will not allow the adventurers to loot it and will fight them if they try. On the desk is a large Elfsteel key which is one of the three Keys of Kelamaz required to reach the summit of Moonspike Tower.

13. Lord's Closet

Shelves along the east wall provide space for neatly folded tunics and hose. A rail along the west wall carries several rotted doublets and shirts. On the south wall is a secret door leading to location 11a (Hard difficulty to detect).

14. Bathing Chamber

This plain chamber has a stone floor. There is a large wooden bath near the south end. From a rail on the wall hang a pair of mouldy green towels. A large jug suitable for pouring water stands in the south-east corner. The bath contains stagnant water at the bottom, at a depth of three centimetres (one inch). Staining around the top of the bath shows that the tub was once filled to a depth of 60 cm (two feet). Dead flies float in the water and the air is rank with the smell: adventurers test Endurance at Standard difficulty or vomit and retch, suffering a level of Fatigue.

15. Mistress' Bedroom

On entering this room the adventurers will notice the scent of rotted flesh. The bed along the north wall is oaken with long drapes surrounding it. Along the west wall, near the door, stands a desk upon which stands a glass jar tipped on its side, with some round pills scattered next to it. Under the jar is a roughly scrawled note in the Dwarven language. A large plush chair sits in the north-east corner. On the bed is a highly-decayed corpse of a Dwarven female, dressed in a rotted dress face-down as if sleeping. The pills can be identified (Hard Lore: Alchemy test, or Standard if performed in a laboratory) as Birchell Root, used for sleeping. The corpse will not animate.

The note reads: "The Dragonmen have come. They have broken the tower gates and my Lord dies at the hand of their commander. I go to join him in our ancestral home. Pray that the foul Necromancer beneath is not set loose."

15a. Mistress' Bathing Room

There is a large ceramic bath in the centre of the floor near the curving south wall of the room. From a rail on the wall hang a pair of rotted blue towels. A large jug suitable for pouring water stands in the south-east corner.

16. Guest's Bedroom

The bed along the north wall is oaken with long drapes surrounding it. Along the east wall, near the door, stands an empty desk. A large plush chair sits in the north-west corner. The bed is neatly made up but full of dust and rotten.

16a. Guest's Bathing Room

This plain chamber has a large ceramic bath in the centre of the floor near the curving south wall of the room. From a rail on the wall hang a pair of rotted green towels. A large jug suitable for pouring water stands in the south-west corner.

17. Barrack Room

These rooms are all similar in appointment: two stacked bunk beds; a chamber pot in a corner; two wooden storage chests. When the complex was attacked, most of the soldiers rallied and fought elsewhere in the Underfort. They left non-essential equipment in these quarters. For variety, there is a 20% chance of each room having some interesting contents. If so, roll 1d6 on the following table but each selection may only be used once. Most of the rooms are otherwise empty.

Barrack Room Discovery Table

1d6	You Discover!
1	TREASURE! 4 CP, 3 SP
2	One Skeleton Shieldguard stands and attacks
3	Shattered Dwarven skeleton and rusted armour with magical Round Shield, +2
4	Headless Dwarven skeleton and magical Chainmail, +1
5	Inanimate Dwarven skeleton lying on the bed wearing Ring of Protection +1, +5% to Resistance Rolls
6	TREASURE! 18 SP, 12 GP, 6 Gems (1 piece of amber 120 GP, 1 fire opal 100 GP, 2 adventurine 50 GP ea., and 2 clear sapphires 15 GP ea.)

18. Store Room

This room contains only the remains of three smashed wooden boxes. Although originally a store room it was looted after the assault.

19. Communal Wash Room

Smashed pottery and broken wooden tubs litter this room, originally used as a communal bathing space. The door to location 20 is closed and swollen stuck (standard Brawn check to force open).

20. Communal Foul Room

Long wooden troughs line the outer curving wall, with oval-shaped holes in the top of each trough's cover. There are spaces for eight persons to sit and relieve themselves. Pipes run into the walls and out of the structure. Unfortunately, the troughs are broken at the bottom and the effluent has flowed onto the floor as damp mud.

21. Communal Foul Room

Long wooden troughs line the outer curving wall, with oval-shaped holes in the top of each trough's cover. There are spaces for eight persons to sit and relieve themselves. Pipes run into the walls. Sitting on one of the troughs is a skeletal Dwarf wearing rusted chainmail armour. A dagger protrudes from his chest, with both hands gripping it tight. His broken spear lies on the floor, the haft having been used to bar the door to location 22. This fellow barred the door and killed himself in an act of cowardice.

22. Communal Wash Room

Eight large water jugs and eight round wooden tubs are placed at intervals around the room, originally used as a communal bathing space. The door to location 21 is closed and barred with a propped spear haft on the other side (Hard Brawn check to force open).

23. Store Room

This room is empty.

Underfort Level 3

24. Grand Banquet Hall

Tattered banners hang from the walls. At the far end of the entry corridor, directly opposite the throne, is the North Stair spiralling up to location 9 and location 2b. Long banquet tables covered in golden plates and goblets form a U-shape; a fine banquet table that hosts the Lord's throne stands at the centre point. Benches run along the sides of the tables. Sitting at the benches are six Skeleton Shieldguards: they died defending the Hall and have been raised by Kelamaz to defend his tomb. They will rise, ready their shields and weapons, and then attack intruders.

Behind the throne stand two ornate stone doors (10 AP, 50 HP) upon which are inscribed the names of the Dwarven warriors who fell at the Battle of Moonspike Tower. Above the doorway are inscribed Dwarven runes which read: "Let none disturb their eternal watch over the tomb of the Necromancer." The doors have been barred on this side using crude wooden planks propped against them.

25. Tomb Access Tunnel

The doors to the Grand Banquet Hall have been barred on the other side, making them two grades more difficult to bash down from inside. Against the walls here are slumped the skeletal remains

of three Dwarves, their skulls smashed. Frescos depicting an army of Dwarven spearmen line each side of the corridor. Along the walls, halfway between the floor and the ceiling, are Dwarven runes. The west wall reads: "And they shall not slumber, those who guard the tomb of Kelamaz." The east wall reads: "Their souls burn, warding the tomb lest the power of evil shall rise once more." The stairway at the south end spirals down to location 32 and location 35.

26. West Kitchen

This room feels noticeably cooler than those nearby. On the curved west wall stands a large fireplace over which hang pots and a large spit, the latter with a long-since rotted animal carcass hanging loose and skeletal. On the trestle tables running through the centre of the room is an amorphous clutter of silver and clay dishes and plates, all covered in Brown Mould.

Brown Mould: Those that move within 1.5 meters (five feet) of a patch of brown mould require an Endurance roll or suffer the loss of one level of Fatigue. This continues if they remain within range. Those that succumb to this loss of body heat can find themselves quickly losing consciousness, where death will quickly follow. A ring of warmth would provide the wearer with complete protection from this fungus. Heat causes brown mould to spread at a rapid rate. Typically, brown mould will increase in size equal to the fire's Intensity x2. See Classic Fantasy page 247 for full details.

Treasure: Underneath the Brown Mould are useable silver plates and dishes worth 500 SP when cleaned up.

27. East Kitchen

On the curved east wall stands a large fireplace over which hang pots and a large empty spit. On the trestle tables running through the centre of the room is an amorphous clutter of clay dishes and plates, many of which are stacked chest high.

28. Well Room

The room is damp and the stone floor is wet with the moisture that permeates the air. The well is the main feature, but a series of eight pipes run down from the ceiling and then bend inwards to proceed down the well. There is a one metre (three foot) circular stone wall around the well hole, which itself descends approximately 12 metres (40 feet) at a 30-degree angle towards the south-east; it runs through the wall and connects to an aqueduct which provides fresh water from Lake Mirrormere.

29. Cold Store

The room is cold and was used as a meat storage room. The carcasses on the hooks long ago rotted away, leaving just the animal bones on the floor.

30. Dry Store

This was the dry store, with raised pallets along the east wall which were used to store dry goods such as flour or rice. The pallets are dried out and fragile, unable to support much weight. The dust is the remains of flour.

31. Ale Store

Broken glass on the floor indicates dropped wine bottles. Three barrels of ale are several hundred years old and spoiled; adventurers drinking some ale will need to test Endurance (Standard difficulty) or vomit and suffer one level of fatigue.

Underfort Level 4 (Cairns)

This cairn features a series of hand-dug 1.5 metre (five foot) wide tunnels and tombs. Battle brothers who were given proper burial rites are immune to necromantic magic. Eight Skeleton Shieldguards have been animated and are stationed by Kelamaz to deter accessing the tombs. The waiting skeletons can be found at each corner of the cairn tunnels, activating when adventurers approach them. These skeletons are the remains of the Dwarves who withdrew into the cairns during the assault above and were sealed in by the Dragonmen, leaving them to their doom. As these skeletons were not properly interred, they are being utilised by the Lich.

The Dwarven Tombs

Use the table below to discover the grave goods associated with an unlabelled tomb – roll 2d6. Adventurers must succeed at a Hard Brawn check to break in; a crowbar makes it 1 step easier. All the tombs contain the skeletons of two Dwarven warriors, interred with their weapons, a round shield each, and wearing their armour.

Unless the grave goods table indicates a magic item, the armour and weapons will be rusted or rotted beyond use.

32. The South Stair

This spiral staircase connects location 25 above with location 35 below. A Skeleton Shieldguard is standing at the base of the stairs at the corner, three metres (10 feet) from the stairwell itself. It will animate when the adventurers step into the cairn passage.

33. The Grand Tomb

Eighteen tombs are gathered into one huge burial chamber containing the lower-caste warriors. Use the Grave Goods table but roll 2d6-2 instead. The secret door in the south wall is well-hidden (Hard difficulty Perception roll, and only if actively searching).

34. The Priest's Tomb

Two tombs stand side-by-side containing the interred remains of four Dwarven Ancestor-Priests. Each body has two white opal gems, one in each eye socket (500 GP each), and an amulet containing an active soulstone around the neck. Adventurers can collect and use the soulstones to power the wards that hold Kelamaz in his prison (see the Level Five notes for details).

Underfort Level 5 (Kelamaz's Prison)

This level of the Underfort was constructed as a special prison for Kelamaz the Lich. It contains an elaborate series of Soul Lenses which are becoming exhausted, each one's failure breaking one of the sacred seals that restrain Kelamaz's will and power. Once all five lenses fail, the seals will all be broken and the Lich will be free to

Dwarven Tombs Grave Goods Table

2d6	Grave Goods include...
2	Four blue spinel gems, two in each Dwarven skull (100 GP each).
3	Four moonstone gems, two in each Dwarven skull (50 GP each).
4	Four electrum coins, two on each Dwarven skull (4 EP), plus a small earthen pot containing 4d6 SP.
5	Four gold coins, two on each Dwarven skull (4 GP).
6	Four electrum coins, two on each Dwarven skull (4 EP).
7	Nothing Special
8	Four silver coins, two on each Dwarven skull (4 SP).
9	Four electrum coins, two on each Dwarven skull (4 EP), plus a small earthen pot containing 2d8 GP.
10	Four fire opal gems, two in each Dwarven skull (100 GP each), plus a magical Great Hammer +1.
11	Four amber gems, two in each Dwarven skull (100 GP each), plus a magical Round Shield +2
12	Four white opal gems, two in each Dwarven skull (1000 GP each), plus a magical Chainmail shirt +1 (Chest and Abdomen).

leave his prison. The primary goal of the adventurers is to restore the Soul Lenses before they all fail.

The Soul Lenses, marked on the map with the letters A through E, each power a sacred seal. Depending on how much time has elapsed, one or more seals will be broken – see the Timeline of Kelamaz's Escape on page 3. To restore each seal the adventurers must access the relevant room, remove the shattered soulstone, and replace it with a charged soulstone before time runs out.

Doors, Soul Lenses, and the Seals

All the doors are made of stone and locked using an intricate internal mechanism. Each door has a triangular key slot and can only be unlocked with the specific key. No attempt can be made to pick the locks (Formidable nonetheless) unless a way can be made to access the mechanism inside the stone door (24 AP, 150 HP).

Appearing as huge oval glass discs, the Soul Lenses have a single soulstone in the centre – a shard of glass-like crystal which glows blue when healthy; these appear blackened and burned as they are exhausted. The energy is projected in a straight line towards the phylactery. A blue sphere emanates around the dais in the centre of the circle. As each Soul Lens fails, the seal at the base of the dais opposite that lens breaks and turns dark. Once a soulstone is replaced in a Soul Lens the energy projection resumes and the seal is restored, glowing blue.

35. The South Stair

The spiral staircase connects location 32 and location 25 above. Two statues of Ancestor-Priests in robes flank the stairs, each pointing their left arm directly leftward. This is to indicate the correct way worshippers at the shrine are expected to walk around the site in a clockwise direction. Adventurers who complete one turn of the route clockwise, stopping to honour all the statues along the way with a bow, receive the blessing of a bonus Luck Point as a reward. This Luck Point is usable once and then depleted. A locked door stands opposite the stairs.

36. The High Priest's Tomb

A single tomb and four statues stand in this area. The statues are of Dwarven Ancestor-Priests, all pointing with their left hand leftward, directing worshippers to walk clockwise. The tomb is ornate and made of stone. It contains a single Dwarven skeleton of the High Priest who sacrificed his own life to power the first crystal once the cairn was constructed. On top of the tomb, protruding vertically, is the key required to open the door to location 39. The tomb itself can be opened if adventurers succeed at a Hard Brawn check (Standard if using a crowbar or similar), and contains the bones of the High Priest; around his neck is a large Elfsteel key, one of the three

Keys of Kelamaz. Surrounding the tomb stand five Skeleton Shield-guards stationed by Kelamaz to stop anyone taking the key.

Kelamaz's Offer: Adventurers reaching this point are tempted by Kelamaz. The whispering voice of Kelamaz offers the character with the lowest Willpower score a place within the necromancer's court in return for breaking the remaining seals. This could be role-played or involve an opposed test of Willpower, at your discretion. Characters with the Good passion can augment the test. The Skeleton Shieldguards attack should the adventurers reject the offer or overcome the character who falls to temptation.

37. Western Ancestor Tomb

The door to the chamber can be opened using the key found in location 39. The room contains two tombs, each of which contains the remains of one Dwarven Ancestor-Priest. Protruding vertically from each tomb is a single glowing blue soulstone which can be removed without difficulty. The tombs can each be opened by adventurers succeeding at a Hard Brawn check (Standard if using a crowbar or similar), but contain only bones.

38. Eastern Ancestor Tomb

The door to the chamber can be opened using the key found in location 41. The room contains two tombs, each of which contains the remains of one Dwarven Ancestor-Priest. Protruding vertically from each tomb is a single glowing blue soulstone which can be removed without difficulty. The tombs can each be opened by adventurers succeeding at a Hard Brawn check (Standard if using a crowbar or similar), but contain only bones.

39. Soul Lens A

The door can be opened using the key found in location 36. The soulstone in the lens will have failed, appearing blackened and shattered. Protruding from the wall to the right of the lens is a stone key which will open the door to location 37. Protruding from the wall to the left of the lens is a stone key that will open the door to location 40.

40. Soul Lens B

The door can be opened using the key found in location 39. The soulstone in the lens is likely to have failed. Protruding from the wall to the left of the lens is a stone key that will open the door to location 41.

41. Soul Lens C

The door can be opened using the key found in location 40. The soulstone in the lens might have failed. Protruding from the wall to the right of the lens is a stone key which will open the door to location 38. Protruding from the wall to the left of the lens is a stone key that will open the door to location 42.

42. Soul Lens D

The door can be opened using the key found in location 41. The soulstone in the lens may have failed. Protruding from the wall to the left of the lens is a stone key that will open the door to location 43.

43. Soul Lens E

The door can be opened using the key found in location 42. Given the timeline of events, the soulstone in the lens is unlikely to have failed and appears blue. Protruding from the wall to the right of the lens is a stone key which will open the door to location 44. Protruding from the wall to the left of the lens is a stone key that will open the door to location 45.

44. Prison Anteroom

The door can be opened using the key found in location 43. There isn't much reason for the adventurers to open it unless they choose to free and then confront Kelamaz directly. The room is bare and features only the outer door to location 45.

45. Kelamaz's Prison

The door can be opened using the key found in location 43. The dais is raised 1.5 metres (five feet) above the stone floor; in the centre stands Kelamaz's adamantine phylactery. Around the lower steps are some other treasures, all contained by the five seals. Only if all five seals are broken can either the adventurers access the treasures or Kelamaz escape.

Treasure: Broadsword of Soul-stealing; Bracers of Defence 5; Kelamaz's Spellbook. The latter is left to the imagination of the Games Master to fill with spells, all written in an ancient dialect of an unknown tongue.

Conclusion

Hopefully the adventurers restore the broken seals. In this instance, they will be able to re-seal the tomb and it will hold Kelamaz for another 1000 years. Should word get out about the place, other adventurers may seek to plunder it, providing future adventures. Alternatively, the adventurers may embark on a quest to discover a means to destroy the Lich's phylactery.

By restoring the prison the adventurers will have impressed Lord Anminster. He is likely to enlist them to lead an assault on Moonspike Tower to remove the Goblin bandits once and for all. Such endeavours are likely to even reach the ears of the King at Sharna.

Failing adventurers will face a terrible death at the hand of Kelamaz unless they flee. The Lich will ignore them unless they actively assault him or otherwise try to resist. He will enslave the village of Anminster. Kelamaz will return to Moonspike Tower and work to conquer the realm of Mystamyr, and eventually all of Greymoor, opening many possibilities for the defeated adventurers.

Statistics

Lord Jared Anminster

Jared is afraid. He knows that the Goblins at Moonspike need dealing with but he is worried that asking for King Jorell's help will weaken his place at court. Jared is not a coward, but he is against violence and does not want any more of his loyal subjects to die. The idea of hiring mercenary adventurers is only just dawning on him as an option.

Lord Jared Anminster		
Action Points: 2		
Damage Modifier: None		
Magic Points: 11		
Movement: 6 metres (20 feet)		
Initiative Bonus: +12 (−7 for armour) = +5		
Armour: Plate mail and chainmail with a steel helm		
Abilities: None		
Magic: None		

1d20	Location	AP/HP
1–3	Right Leg	5/5
4–6	Left Leg	5/5
7–9	Abdomen	8/6
10–12	Chest	8/7
13–15	Right Arm	5/4
16–18	Left Arm	5/4
19–20	Head	8/5

Skills

Athletics 52%, Brawn 54%, Deceit 44%, Endurance 52%, Evade 52%, Insight 54%, Languages (Common Tongue) 64%, Locale (Mystamyr) 66%, Perception 44%, Stealth 44%, Unarmed 42%, Willpower 42%

Passions

Good (Lawful, Pacifistic) 62%, Loyal to King Jorell of Sharna 74%

Combat Style & Weapons

Human Knight (Sword and Shield) 52%

Weapon	Size/Force	Reach	Damage	AP/HP
Round Shield	*L*	*S*	*1d4*	*4/12*
Broadsword	*M*	*M*	*1d8*	*6/10*

Sgt Daymond Yarnek, Acting Warden

Acting Warden ever since Janus Elias went missing two weeks ago, Yarnek wants to destroy the Goblins at Moonspike Tower. He's frustrated with Lord Anminster and suspicious of mercenaries, who he sees as mere sell-swords. If the adventurers impress him, however, he'll happily support their use to defeat the Moonspike Goblins.

Sergeant Yarnek		
Action Points: 2		
Damage Modifier: None		
Magic Points: 11		
Movement: 6 metres (20 feet)		
Initiative Bonus: +12 (−5 for armour) = +7		
Armour: Chainmail and studded leather with a steel helm		
Abilities: None		
Magic: None		

1d20	Location	AP/HP
1–3	Right Leg	3/5
4–6	Left Leg	3/5
7–9	Abdomen	5/6
10–12	Chest	5/7
13–15	Right Arm	3/4
16–18	Left Arm	3/4
19–20	Head	8/5

Skills

Athletics 52%, Brawn 54%, Deceit 44%, Endurance 62%, Evade 62%, Insight 54%, Languages (Common Tongue) 64%, Locale (Mystamyr) 66%, Perception 44%, Stealth 44%, Unarmed 52%, Willpower 52%

Passions

Good (Adheres to Tradition) 52%, Loyal to Lord Anminster 64%

Combat Style & Weapons

Human Soldier (Bow, Spear and Shield) 62%

Weapon	Size/Force	Reach	Damage	AP/HP
Round Shield	*L*	*S*	*1d4*	*4/12*
Shortspear	*M*	*L*	*1d8+1*	*4/5*
Short Bow	*L*	*–*	*1d6*	*4/4*

Relgan Lothbeer, Inn Proprietor

Relgan is the Dwarven proprietor of The Slaughtered Ettin. The stout and loud landlord is well-renowned for his tall stories of adventures from his famed "early days" as an adventurer. In fact, Relgan is a congenital liar who merrily steals tales from actual adventurers and adapts them to his own narrative. This makes him an outstanding story-teller. He is, nonetheless, a brave villager who will stand with the adventurers against the undead.

Relgan Lothbeer
Action Points: 2
Damage Modifier: +1d2
Magic Points: 11
Movement: 4 metres (15 feet)
Initiative Bonus: +12 (−5 for armour) = +7
Armour: Chainmail and studded leather with a steel helm
Abilities: Magic Resistance, Poison Resistance, Infravision, Tunnel Sense
Magic: None

1d20	Location	AP/HP
1–3	Right Leg	3/6
4–6	Left Leg	3/6
7–9	Abdomen	5/7
10-12	Chest	5/8
13–15	Right Arm	3/5
16–18	Left Arm	3/5
19–20	Head	8/6

Skills

Athletics 47%, Brawn 56%, Craft (Metallurgy) 54%, Craft (Masonry) 54%, Customs 76%, Deceit 52%, Endurance 62%, Evade 42%, Insight 44%, Languages (Common Tongue and Dwarvish) 64%, Locale (Mystamyr) 66%, Lore (Underdeep) 56%, Perception 54%, Stealth 44%, Survival 47%, Unarmed 57%, Willpower 42%

Passions

Neutral (Dishonest, Vain) 52%

Combat Style & Weapons

Dwarven Warrior (Axe, Hammer, and Shield) 57%

Weapon	Size/Force	Reach	Damage	AP/HP
Round Shield	L	S	1d4+1d2	4/12
Blood Axe	H	L	2d6+2+1d2	4/10

Blood Axe is a magical great axe and glows a deep orange-red when evil creatures are nearby.

Warhammer	M	M	1d8+1+1d2	3/8

Kelamaz, Lich Necromancer of Ettinmarsh, Rank 5

The Lich Necromancer Kelamaz was born to an elven family in the city of Imras. Having developed a talent for arcane magic, he left home seeking lost tomes and learning many secrets. Using a magical portal he constructed, Kelamaz travelled to realms unknown and returned as an immortal Lich. Defeated by the Dwarves of Zirazund, he seeks revenge.

Special Notes:

- *The lich's touch inflicts damage directly to an opponent's hit points and ignores any worn mundane armour; magic armour offers protection equal to the magic bonus. Once touched, an opponent that suffers even 1 point of damage must succeed at an Opposed roll comparing their Willpower to that of the lich or suffer paralysis, being held on the spot.*

- *The lich becomes immune to most non-magical attacks, its bones instantly re-knitting together.*

Kelamaz, Lich Necromancer of Ettinmarsh

Action Points: 4

Damage Modifier: +0

Magic Points: 16

Movement: 4 metres (15 feet)

Initiative Bonus: +20

Luck Points: 8

Armour: Supernaturally strong bones and mummified flesh

Abilities: Dark Sight, Immunity (Charm, Sleep, Enfeeblement, Polymorph, Cold, Electricity, Insanity, and Death spells), Intensity 21, Terrifying, and Undead

Magic/Spells Memorized: Mass Charm*, Meteor Shower,* Time Stop*, Control Weather*, Death Spell*, Globe of Invulnerability*, Invisible Stalker*, Word of Power – Kill*, Monster Summoning – Greater*, True Seeing*, Animate Dead, Charm Monster, Dimension Door, Hail/Ice Storm, Illusionary Terrain, Invisibility – Greater, Polymorph Self, Bestow Curse, Darkness, Dispel Magic, Fireball, Fly, Hold Person, Know Passions, Lightning Bolt, Locate Object, Mage Lock, Slow, plus 12 Rank 1 spells of Games Master's choice.

See Classic Fantasy Expert Set

1d20	Location	AP/HP
1–3	Right Leg	6/7
4–6	Left Leg	6/7
7–9	Abdomen	6/8
10-12	Chest	6/9
13–15	Right Arm	6/6
16–18	Left Arm	6/6
19–20	Head	6/7

Skills

Arcane Casting 132%, Arcane Knowledge 132%, Athletics 59%, Brawn 65%, Deceit 60%, Endurance 84%, Evade 78%, Insight 102%, Languages (Common, Elven, Dwarvish, Dragon Tongue, Goblin) 60%, Perception 92%, Stealth 71%, Unarmed 59%, Willpower 112%

Passions

Lawful (Close-minded, Judgmental, and Lack of Adaptability) 102%, Evil (Cruel and Hate Good) 102%, Thirst for Knowledge 102%

Combat Style & Weapons

Touch of Death (Clawed Hand) 69%

Weapon	Size/Force	Reach	Damage	AP/HP
Clawed Hand	S	T	1d6 plus paralysis	As for Arm

Anminster Guard/Militiaman

Anminster Militia

Action Points: 2

Damage Modifier: None

Magic Points: 11

Movement: 6 metres (20 feet)

Initiative Bonus: +12 (–5 for armour) = +7

Armour: Chainmail and studded leather with a steel helm

Abilities: None

Magic: None

1d20	Location	AP/HP
1–3	Right Leg	3/5
4–6	Left Leg	3/5
7–9	Abdomen	5/6
10-12	Chest	5/7
13–15	Right Arm	3/4
16–18	Left Arm	3/4
19–20	Head	8/5

Skills

Athletics 52%, Brawn 54%, Deceit 44%, Endurance 52%, Evade 52%, Insight 54%, Languages (Common Tongue) 64%, Locale (Mystamyr) 66%, Perception 44%, Stealth 44%, Unarmed 42%, Willpower 42%

Passions

Neutral (Egotistic) 52%, Loyal to Lord Anminster 54%

Combat Style & Weapons

Human Soldier (Bow, Spear and Shield) 52%

Weapon	Size/Force	Reach	Damage	AP/HP
Round Shield	L	S	1d4	4/12
Shortspear	M	L	1d8+1	4/5
Short Bow	L	–	1d6	4/4

Skeleton, Human

Human Skeleton		
Action Points: 3		
Damage Modifier: None		
Magic Points: 2		
Movement: 6 metres (20 feet)		
Initiative Bonus: +13		
Armour: None		
Abilities: Immunity (Fear, Sleep, and Charm), Intensity 1, Undead		
Magic: None		

1d20	Location	AP/HP
1–3	Right Leg	0/4
4–6	Left Leg	0/4
7–9	Abdomen	0/5
10-12	Chest	0/6
13–15	Right Arm	0/3
16–18	Left Arm	0/3
19–20	Head	0/4

Skills

Athletics 56%, Brawn 52%, Endurance 44%, Evade 64%, Perception 40%, Unarmed 56%, Willpower 34%

Combat Style & Weapons

Skeletal Warrior (Sword, Spear, and/or Shield) 56%

Weapon	Size/Force	Reach	Damage	AP/HP
Short Spear	M	L	1d8+1	4/5
Target Shield	L	S	1d4	4/12
Short Sword	M	S	1d6	6/8

Zombie, Human

Zombie		
Action Points: 2		
Damage Modifier: +1d2		
Magic Points: 2		
Movement: three metres (10 feet)		
Initiative Bonus: +8		
Armour: None		
Abilities: Immunity (Fear, Sleep, and Charm), Intensity 2, Undead		
Magic: None		

1d20	Location	AP/HP
1–3	Right Leg	0/6
4–6	Left Leg	0/6
7–9	Abdomen	0/7
10-12	Chest	0/8
13–15	Right Arm	0/5
16–18	Left Arm	0/5
19–20	Head	0/6

Skills

Athletics 54%, Brawn 60%, Endurance 64%, Perception 40%, Unarmed 54%, Willpower 34%

Combat Style & Weapons

Mindless Undead Pummelling (Bite and Claws) 54%

Weapon	Size/Force	Reach	Damage	AP/HP
Bite	S	S	1+1d2	As for Head
Fists	S	T	1d3+1d2	As for Arm

Skeleton Shieldguard, Dwarven

Dwarven Shieldguards are the animated remains of those Dwarven warriors buried in tombs or cairns and then raised by foul necromancy. Buried in their armour and with their weapons, Skeleton Guardians are a dread challenge for new adventurers.

Skeleton Shieldguard		
Action Points: 3		
Damage Modifier: None		
Magic Points: 2		
Movement: 4 metres (15 feet)		
Initiative Bonus: +7 (−7 for armour)		
Armour: Plate armoured breastplate and helm with chainmail on limbs		
Abilities: Immunity (Fear, Sleep, and Charm), Intensity 1, Undead		
Magic: None		

1d20	Location	AP/HP
1–3	Right Leg	5/5
4–6	Left Leg	5/5
7–9	Abdomen	7/6
10-12	Chest	7/7
13–15	Right Arm	5/4
16–18	Left Arm	5/4
19–20	Head	7/5

Skills

Athletics 60%, Brawn 54%, Endurance 50%, Evade 64%, Perception 42%, Unarmed 60%, Willpower 34%

Combat Style & Weapons

Skeletal Warrior (Choose two or three from the following: Axe, Hammer, Sword, Dagger, Mace, Spear, Shield) 60%

Weapon	Size/Force	Reach	Damage	AP/HP
Broadsword	*M*	*M*	*1d8*	*6/10*
Warhammer	*M*	*M*	*1d8+1*	*3/8*
Dagger	*S*	*S*	*1d4+1*	*6/8*
Horseman's Mace	*M*	*S*	*1d8*	*6/6*
Round Shield	*L*	*S*	*1d4*	*4/12*
Shortspear	*M*	*L*	*1d8+1*	*4/5*

Karden Nord, Haunt

Karden is the spirit of the defeated Dwarven Lord of Warrior's Eyrie. He haunts the Underfort and might meet the adventurers. To lay his soul to rest, the adventurers must return his skull from the Fire Citadel of the Dragon Kings.

Karden Nord
INT: 14
POW: 13
CHA: 16
Abilities: Intensity 2, Telekinesis, Possession, Deathly Touch, Glamour, Wither
Skills: Spectral Combat 59%, Languages (Common, Dwarvish, Dragon Tongue) 60%, Lore (Memories of Defeat) 58%, Willpower 76%
Passions: Good (Adheres to Tradition) 56%, Protect Karden Nord's Remains 59%, Stand Vigil over Kelamaz 57%
Abilities: Immunity (Fear, Sleep, and Charm), Intensity 1, Undead
Magic: None